T0113526

Zimbolicious Poetry Anthology:

Volume 2

Edited by **Tendai Rinos Mwanaka**
Edward Dzonze

Mwanaka Media and Publishing Pvt Ltd,
Chitungwiza Zimbabwe
*
Creativity, Wisdom and Beauty

Publisher: *Mmap*
Mwanaka Media and Publishing Pvt Ltd
24 Svosve Road, Zengeza 1
Chitungwiza Zimbabwe
mwanaka@yahoo.com
mwanaka13@gmail.com
https://www.mmapublishing.org
www.africanbookscollective.com/publishers/mwanaka-media-and-publishing
https://facebook.com/MwanakaMediaAndPublishing/

Distributed in and outside N. America by African Books Collective
orders@africanbookscollective.com
www.africanbookscollective.com

ISBN: 978-1-77925-581-5
EAN: 9781779255815

© Tendai Rinos Mwanaka 2021

All rights reserved.
No part of this book may be reproduced or transmitted in any form or by any
means, mechanical or electronic, including photocopying and recording, or be
stored in any information storage or retrieval system, without written
permission from the publisher

DISCLAIMER
All views expressed in this publication are those of the author and do not
necessarily reflect the views of *Mmap*.

Table of Contents

About Editors...vi

Contributors Bio Notes.................................vii

Introduction..xii

Desire To Read From Udomorophobia: *Chenjerai Mhondera*...1

1-9: *Tendai Rinos Mwanaka*.............................2

Weaving Away the Poetry Basket (2): *Jackson Tendai Matimba*...5

Poetry Of Change: *Killian Mwanaka*.................9

Dear commissar: *Mbizo Chirasha*...................11

Poetry: *Elizabeth Semende*..........................12

My Heart Cries: *Lovers Pamire*.....................14

My Foot: *Learnmore Edwin Zvada*.................15

Ndabaikana!: *Shadreck Matindike*..................16

She Tickled my Fancy!: *Shadreck Matindike*......17

All in good time: *Lisa Jaison*......................18

Buried Dreams: *Constance van Niekerk*...........20

When The Lights Went Out: *Troy da Costa*........21

A Journey: *Tavonga Maipe*..........................22

I watched the rose wilt and die: *Thamsanqa Wuna*.....24

Your absence puts me in another world: *Hosea Tokwe*....26

A Smile For Things To Come Stood Tall: *Cosmas Shoko*.....27

How much you mean to me: *Hosea Tokwe*..........28

Do not blame the Mirror: *Albert Nyathi*..........30

Ego Protector: *Lisa Jaison*.........................31

The Guilty Trip: *Tendai Rinos Mwanaka*...........35

Mount Hampden: *Patricia D. Dube*................37

To My Mother-In-Law: *Robson Isaac Shoes Lambada*.....38

Lamentations: *Nellah Nonkondlo Mtanenhlabathi*.......40

Broken Future: *Jurgen Martin Namupira*...........41

Bars: *Constance van Niekerk*.......................42

Resilience: *Albert Nyathi*...........................43

untitled short poem: *Cosmas Shoko*...............43

iii

Nkunkumina YaBinga: *Aleck Nchite Munkuli*....................*44*
The Lion Of Binga: *Aleck Nchite Munkuli (translation)*...........*47*
Today is their day (Heroes' Day): *Edward Dzonze*.............*49*
You were there: *Chido J. Ndoro*...................................*52*
Forgive them Nyongolo:. *Nellah Nonkondlo Mtanenhlabathi*.....*54*
Murder Most Foul: *Jabulani Mzinyathi*............................*56*
Africa; To whom it may concern: *Edward Dzonze*..............*57*
Kaddafi: *Mbizo Chirasha*..*59*
Am not black, but an African: *Lovers Pamire*.....................*60*
Black Oranges: *Mbizo Chirasha*...................................*62*
The Woes of My Color: *Debra Chimuka*..........................*66*
African Footprints: *Constance van Niekerk*........................*68*
Childhood memories of Nyachuru River: *Edward Dzonze*....*70*
A Prize for the Black Eye: *Hosea Tokwe*.........................*72*
AIDS: *Elizabeth Semende*...*73*
The storm: *Phumulani Chipandambira*.............................*75*
The setting sun: *Jabulani Mzinyathi*...............................*76*
A Rural Woman: *Lovers Pamire*...................................*77*
Mukadzi wekuna Zvirevo 31: *Shadreck Matindike*..............*79*
The Wife of Proverbs 31: *Shadreck Matindike*....................*80*
Beautiful woman: *Tavonga Maipe*.................................*82*
The missing person: *Phumulani Chipandambira*...................*84*
Another day: *Jabulani Mzinyathi*...................................*85*
The Wretched Of The Earth: *Killian Mwanaka*................*86*
Electioneering: *Robson Isaac Shoes Lambada*.....................*87*
Annihilation's edge: *Patricia D. Dube*.............................*88*
Confessions of a war veteran: *Robson Isaac Shoes Lambada*......*89*
What Next?: *Killian Mwanaka*.....................................*91*
Uhleko lolu ngolwani?: *Tembi Charles*.............................*93*
What is this laughter?: *Tembi Charles (translation)*.................*94*
Gudo guru petamuswe: *David W Mwanaka*.......................*95*
Old Baboon, fold your tail:. *David W Mwanaka (translation by
Tendai Mwanaka)*... ....*97*

iv

Predicament: *Thamsanqa Wuna*.....................................*99*
The House We Sold: *Troy da Costa*.............................*100*
Chitungwiza Map (Redraft): *Phumulani Chipandambira*........*101*
Journey Home: *Anesu Nyakubaya*...............................*102*
Mother: *Tembi Charles*.....................................*103*
Yahwe: *Kelvin Mangwende*.....................................*105*
The Mad Man: *Kelvin Mangwende*...............................*105*
In the Land of the Lucid: *Debra Chimuka*......................*106*
Karara: *Kelvin Mangwende*.....................................*109*
Fallen Leaf: *Kelvin Mangwende*...............................*109*
Cancel: *Chenjerai Mhondera*...................................*110*
Ndaisaiva kuti ndiwo hupenyu: *Kelvin Mangwende*............*111*
Not Knowing This Is Life: *Kelvin Mangwende*..................*111*
On Spring Night: *Learnmore Edwin Zvada*......................*112*
This is my Home: Sands of Time: *Tendai Rinos Mwanaka*....*113*
Mmap New African Poets Series............................*116*

v

About Editors

Tendai Rinos Mwanaka is an editor, writer, visual artist and musical artist with 10 individual books and 5 edited anthologies published which include among others, *Zimbolicious Poetry Anthology, Playing To Love's Gallery, Keys in the River, Voices from Exile, Counting The Stars,* and many more here *http://www.africanbookscollective.com/authors-editors/tendai-rinos-mwanaka.* He writes in English and Shona. His work has appeared in over 400 journals and anthologies from over 27 countries. Work has been translated into Spanish, French and German.

EDWARD DZONZE, 26, is a self made poetry critic and finds his purpose in life through playing around with words. He is the author of *Many Truths Told at Once, Royalty Publishing USA, 2015,* and *Wisdom Speaks, Royalty Publishing USA, 2016.* His poetry has appeared in numerous anthologies including, *We are One, Diaspora Publishers UK, 2014; World peace anthology, India, 2014,* and recently in *Best New African Poets 2015 and 2016 Anthology*

Contributors Bio Notes

Debra Chimuka is an upcoming Zimbabwean writer. She holds a bachelor of arts degree and a human resources management diploma with University of Cape Town

Phumulani Chipandambira is a freelance writer who lives in Norton, Zimbabwe. He likes reading and writing short stories and poems. His works have been published in various local magazines, blogs and newspapers.

Mbizo Chirasha is an acclaimed wordsmith, performances poet, widely published poet and writer. The widely traveled poet and creative projects consultant is published in more than 60 journals, anthologies, websites, reviews, newspapers, blogs and poetry collections around the world. Some of the countries he traveled to include Ghana, Sweden, Egypt, Tanzania, South Africa, Mozambique, Namibia, Zambia and Malawi. He co-authored *Whispering woes of Ganges and Zambezi* with Sweta Vikram from New York in 2010. His poetry collection *Good Morning President* was published by Diaspora publishers UK in 2011.

Troy Da Costa was born 14/10/1978 in Harare Zimbabwe. He now lives in London UK. Notably published in, *Esquire UK*, *Esquire UK online*, *Red online*, *Women's Health UK*. He blogs at: troyfdacosta.blogspot.co.uk

I am **Patricia D. Dube**, born in March 1987, in the city of Kings and Queens, Ko Bulawayo. I have a deep love for poetry and have been writing for more than 10 years. I have published some of my work in two poetry collections

Lisa Jaison:_I was born in the city of Gweru in Zimbabwe. After my first degree at the Midlands State University I relocated to South Africa where I commenced a carrier as a research consultant, and studying for my post grad with the University of South Africa. I remain an avid reader and an artist at heart.

Robson Isaac Shoes Lambada is a writer leading a cultural activists network called the Zimbabwe Poets for Human Rights. He was born in Kadoma and currently lives in Harare. He completed his formal education at Martin Spur Schools and Jameson High School before he went on to study at the Midlands State University. He is a NAMA award nominee for the Outstanding Poet (2013). He has been performing and reading his poetry professionally since 2004. He has travelled to most of the countries in the region with his poetry and beyond the oceans to countries that include Germany, Netherlands and United States of America.

My name is **Tavonga Maipe**. I am 25. I am from Lusulu, Binga. I love writing poems and short stories. None of my work has been published yet. I am currently residing in Cape Town, South Africa.

I am **Kelvin Mangwende**, I have published two Shona plays namely *Chaminuka,* and *Chimurenga (War)* An Anthology of poems called *The madman in Heaven.* I have featured in several anthologies and I have published a collection of short stories called *An axe with a Blood.*

Shadreck Matindike was born on the 8th of September 1985 in Gweru, Zimbabwe. He holds a Bachelor of Commerce Honours Degree in Economics and a Masters Degree in Economics, both from the Midlands State University, Zimbabwe. He is published in areas of Economics, Finance and African literature. He has over 5 years experience teaching covering secondary level up to post-graduate studies. He is attached to Solusi University, Zimbabwe Open University and Government of Zimbabwe.

My name is Jackson **Tendai Matimba**. I was born in Nyanga District in the year 1978. I did primary education at Nyatate primary and secondary education at Dangamvura high in Mutare. I write poetry and novels and my poems also appear in several anthologies including the famous, *Best New African Poets 2015*, which was co-edited by Tendai Mwanaka. Some works include; *The Nature of My Signature*, a poetry book published by Royalty publishingUSA. Currently I am waiting for the publication of my new poetry book entitled, *Weaving Away the Poetry Basket.*

Chenjerai Mhondera is a novelist, poet, performer, playwright, actor and songwriter. He is a patron and founder of Young Writers Club in Mabelreign-Warren Park district. He comes from the Eastern highlands, lives in Zimbabwe and is a citizen of the world.

Aleck 'Nchite' Munkuli was born in 1981 in Binga. He went to Syanzyundu and Tinde High schools. He trained as a teacher at UCE from 2002 – 2005. He also obtained his BEd at UNISA. He is currently teaching in South Africa and also studying towards the Honours.

David W. Mwanaka is formerly a Journalist, he is the first black farmer in the UK, now turned business man. He writes poetry and music

Killian Nhamo Mwanaka was born 12 Jan. 1953, Nyatate, Nyanga. Left Zimbabwe for Botswana to join Zimbabwe African National Liberation Army (ZANLA) forces while in second year of teaching course at United College of Education, Bulawayo in 1973. Was arrested by Mugabe with a group of *Vashandi* in 1976 after objecting to Mugabe's brutality, thrown into underground jails at Chimoio, and Beira jail, released in 1979. Briefly joined Zimbabwe National Army at independence and left to join a progressive co-operative newspaper called *The Vanguard 1984*, was Editor of *Gweru Times* 1988 – 1992, went to Rhodes University for Journalism courses, worked as Information Officer in Somaliland under the United Nations Development Programme 1993 -2000 doing demobilisation, re-integration and rehabilitation of the militia in that country. Left for London in 2001 and is a businessman in London. He was published in the seminal anthology of Zimbabwean poets *Now The Poets Speak* and in *Another Battle Begun*

Jabulani Mzinyathi was born in Gweru, Zimbabwe in Ascot High Density Surburb to working class parents. He calls himself a poet, prophet, philosopher. He is a writer in general and a poet in particular. His works have been published in several anthologies, magazines, ezines in Zimbabwe and abroad. Jabulani is a pan African who is also an internationalist. Jabulani is an avid reader who is a qualified teacher, lawyer and human resources management practitioner. He calls himself an explosion that is an implosion.

Jurgen Martin Namupira was born on 2 May 1996 in Harare, Zimbabwe and raised in Chegutu. Currently he is studying an electronics student at Northlink College in Cape Town, South Africa. He went to David Whitehead primary school and did O level at Chegutu high school and his A level at St Francis high Chegutu. Writing is not a profession for him but a passion driven by talent and is the author of a poetry collection titled GRRETINGS!. His main themes of concern are abuse, love and freedom.

Constance van Niekerk is a South African-based Zimbabwean-born creative writer, poet, music lover, spoken word artist, blogger and educator. She has contributed to several anthologies and published her own poetry collection, *Echoes of My Heart*. Constance is the Editor of two online publications, *ZimOnLineNews* and *AfriqueBeat*. Writing is her passion and blogging her obsession…well just a little bit obsessed!

Chido J. Ndoro is a protest and women's issues poet who has been writing since 2009. She is studying for a Bachelor of Arts Honours Degree in English and Applied Communication. She mainly focuses on protest literature that addresses the political, economic and social issues in Africa. She also addresses women issues, illuminating the difficulties women face in society.

My name is **Anesu Nyakubaya**. I am from Zimbabwe but currently live in South Africa. I love writing. It's like a loudspeaker for my inner voice. It literally gives me wings to fly. When I write all things are possible .My inspiration is drawn from everything I experience and see around me. I was once told that all one needs to do to find inspiration is to concentrate, this is something I try and do with my work. More of my pieces can be viewed on my blog *soulfulmiss.com*

Albert Nyathi is a Poet, Musician, Writer, Actor, Producer, Academic, Philanthropist and Activist. He published 6 books, *The Third Dimension*, with Danish authors 1994, *Echoes from Zimbabwe* - 2010, *My Daughter* - 2012, *My Son* - 2016, co-written with Ignatius Mabasa, *Ten Conversations to End AIDS* - 2016, co-written with Dr. Daniel Low-Beer, *Ten Conversations on Health* - 2016, co-written with Dr. Daniel Low-Beer (current project). He produced the highly acclaimed song "Senzenina" on the album "For How Long?", in 1994 after the assassination of Chris Hani and the song/poem was dedicated to Hani.

Lovers Pamire was born on the 25th of August 1981 in Hurungwe Karoi at a place called Mudzimu. He is an Occupational Health Nurse by profession. He is a Country musician with four albums to his name. Art is his food and drink and he finds satisfaction in it. He is an actor, videographer and editor. He considered seriously taking his poetic skills to another level recently when he made his debut in *Zimbolicious Poetry*

Introduction

"Zimbolicious girl a song by *Prince Tendai Mupfurutsa* in the 1990s brought this word into any form of recording. With the beautiful sultry babes dancing to this new urban beat we extolled the beauty of our unique ladies in Zimbabwe. It is a combination of the word Zimbo, for Zimbabwean, and licious from the English word delicious, thus it talks of the beauty and deliciousness of Zimbabwean girls. We borrowed from this to create our own brand of anthology, *Zimbolicious Poetry*. It is the beauty and deliciousness of Zimbabwe's poetry that we offer in this anthology. In her essay, *Flora Veit-Wild*, for *Seminar für Afrikawissenschaften, Humboldt Universität zu Berlin*, Online, tackles this word literary and writes that, "'Zimbolicious' is a term I picked up from one of the numerous Zimbolingo chat forums that serve Zimbabweans at home and in the diaspora to communicate among one another. Having been coined 'to describe the beauty of Zimbabwean women', for me this exquisite new word is a most suitable epithet for what I want to explore in this essay: the creative energy arising from the mix of languages – the 'delicious pie dish', as South African poet Ike Mboneni Muila calls it, in which 'languages [take] the place of cake flour'." Just like Zimbabwean girls, Zimbabwean poetry is delicious", we wrote in the introduction note to the first Zimbolicious anthology, last year. A year later we are full circle, producing another delicious potpourri of all that is beautiful about Zimbabwean poetry.

Poetry is fragments of music thrown into the air. The primary job and aim of a poet is to create those musical notes, to play those musical notes, and the wind will take those fragment notes, sounds, musics into the ears of listeners. And in an article online,

Unpacking Myths Around Zimbolicious Poetry Anthology and Zimbabwean Writing: Toward a Poet's Vocation by *Tendai Mwanaka*, he dissected what it meant to be a poet, saying. "The whole idea about being a poet is to write, publish and be read… Poets should write to be read, to create culture, to change language, ideas, society. These are the vocations for a serious poet." And how can a poet be read without a wind taking forward their words into the readers' ears!

Zimbolicious is one of these winds among many others. Its job is to transport the musics of the Zimbabwean poets into the ears, hearts and souls of the listeners. As we all are aware of, when the wind travels it has no boundaries, it collects, it deposits, it mixes up things, you never know where that leaf you see the wind carrying will eventually be deposited, is there another wind, another element that is going to move that leaf, to another place. Once something is moved then it is no longer in the control of progenitors of such a thing. It now belongs to the journey and the destination. This is what our intention was in creating and continuing with the Zimbolicious poetry anthologies. We firmly believe it is a good wind. It will be able to push our poetry making in Zimbabwe into other frontiers.

This year's *Zimbolicious Poetry Anthology, Volume 2* continues from where we left with the first *Zimbolicious Poetry Anthology* we created in 2016, so we advise the collectors and readers to also buy the first Zimbolicious to keep the thread, to enjoy the start of this story of Zimbabwe. We have 77 poems from 30 poets and translators, which include among others; experienced poets, academic poets, street poets, emergent poets, beginning poets, all telling stories associated with what all these poets refer to as home, that is, Zimbabwe. It has several stories, several narrative strands, several arguments, agreements, disagreements, acceptances, ideas, beliefs…, all shaped by that place they call Zimbabwe. It is an ongoing debate on what is Zimbabwe, what we want our Zimbabwe to be socially, culturally, politically…, thus we allowed every opinion space in this anthology, whether us editors agree with them or not. We have poets tackling issues to do with poetry, writing in general, art, place, identity, tradition, struggle, culture, gender, collective understanding, religion, individual, human rights and love.

"Knowing how beautiful Zimbabwean poetry is always, this is indeed   a   delicious   dish!"

DESIRE TO READ FROM UDOMOROPHOBIA
CHENJERAI MHONDERA

Let me read from book of Udomorophobia,
Under Mohoroshenene code;
I want to read about deeds of man;
Wisdom of a cunning man;
Archive that keeps art surviving
From fool's tales, I want to hear stories of geniuses who never
writ.
Let me read from book of Udomorophobia,
I want to hear how nonsense written is better than sense not
written.
Let me read from Udomorophobia,
I want to hear how man is a captive of his own fears.
Let me read from Udomorophobia,
For an Honours Degree in Cyquanchura and Antagonism
psychology;
Let me read so fast, I want to spell wisdom with eloquence.
Let me read, I want to hear language corrosive than acid;
The uppercuts and punches of a dissident reporter.
Let me read from the book of Udomorophobia;
I want to hear carefreeness from a liberty mind.
Let me read not so fast, I want to hear about man who fears to
fear!

1-9

Tendai Rinos Mwanaka

The number 1 still bores me like James Mukonoweshuro
James Mukonoweshuro was a student in my primary school
grades
He always got the top spot, in the class, in the grade
Number 1
Always wanting to be the first, negating Zero out of existence, or
even negating negatives…
Negating negatives was not a positive. Thus 1 minus 2…was…*it
can't*
They were no negatives or Zero for me at primary school; to beat
James Mukonoweshuro with.
I was always number 2 or worse
2 attracted me, even now. Its angles and curves
I hated 3, because
It wasn't closer to number 1, like 2 was
It was good to know that even though he was always number 1,
he could feel me at number 2
Number 3 and he would just ignore me
The U in four (4), is yes, gives me voluptuous pleasure. Which u?
You!
Are you asking me?
I love 5, even though if you were to twist one side of it, it would
look like 3, the 3 I hated
Twisted untwisted, and twisted…is it crazy? Is 5 a normal twin of
an abnormal 3?
But 5 represent freedom (who is saying that!), adaptability (due to
the twisting and untwisting twists), unpredictable travel (in the
Himalaya mountains.), and abuses of senses (when it is 3); it is 5.
Who is twisting it? It depends with whose hand(s)

Six (6)…and did he say sex…has always been interesting
It looks like an abnormal…I mean, upside down thing swimming
off, to fertilize…populate her with abnormality. Pregnancy…. It's
like my father was a virgin when he met my mother. So mine was
a virgin birth, even though I am the second born…was the
second born
I can't be the second born now
I am not in a state of perpetual birth
I can't say the second alive, to live
I stop it!
7 is boring, just like some joined kindling, or an axe, chopping off
things…like on a news clip when the demented character gets
hold of an axe and starts chomping off limps…of people, at a
vacation outing, in the deep forests of Mississippi , as they try to
flee from his axe, and call the police
It's his axe, oozing out Mississippi blood. Blue
And we watch it on the news; it is like in one of those movies.
We are supposed to feel sorry for these people, but we had been
told people on the television do not die
Did they catch the guy?
Nope, it is cold case
Seven is a lot of humanity, to die from an axe
It's his axe
And we were supposed to feel empathy
Seven is just too cold, seven hells, seventh hell?
It is seven with a small bar on its middle 7, that's a bit interesting
If you twist this one, it becomes 4
You are asking me how, really!
Sorry, I can't answer you for the sanatorium in my head (heart)
has (or even soul)
77777777777777777777777777777777777777777777777777777777
7777777 beds

I mean 7 beds. The first one is for James Mukonoweshuro, mine is the second one, the third one is for you, and that's why you are reading this. The forth one has a patient in it and he is the only one physically there, a patient who is not a patient, the fifth one has a shadow in it, twisting and twisting, retilting the twists like 5. The sixth one is for your woman, girl or whatever you call her, the seventh one is an object, I mean Chinese food: dogs or snakes meat

8 is curvy. It is the most interesting number, with its sexy curves, booming out. It encloses things in its two curves

It's not inside its two circles where I would want to be, but outside of it…licking its curves…

Licking and licking ice cream

9 is a 6 raised to a standing position. Might not be as productive as sex because the tail swims off rightly, the right way….

The correct way

That is

The right way

Words!

No…

Numbers?

Maybe

Weaving Away the Poetry Basket (2)

Jackson Tendai Matimba

The girl is weaving, she weaves a poetry basket
She weaves with imported material that she mix with indigenous
materials
Weaving the bread basket of poetry
She weaves in black, she weaves in white; she weaves in black and
white
Mixing together all bright colours for the poetry basket
Every night she is weaving, weaving by the fireside
Alone in the sitting room by the candlelight she surely is weaving
Weaving profusely the poetry basket
She weaves by the streetlight the moonlight and the starlight
And under the heavy spell of the creation
In her heavy pregnancy she is weaving the poetry basket
Weaving off with tears of joy, she weaves all year round
She weaves a poetry basket; for the use of a bread basket
She weaves ahead of the harvest; she weaves for the vegetable
markets
It is a poetry basket with a heavy lid that she is weaving
Which grows big like the grain silos of the whole nation
From her youth, she weaves; she is weaving in her olden days she
is weaving
She is weaving right to her death, as she kicks her last throes
She weaves and weaves; yes she must weave
It is a poetry basket that she weaves
She weaves like a Nigerian, she is weaving like in a fairy-tale
Even in her troubled sleep and her sweet dreams; she is weaving

The boy is riding, he rides a poetry horse
He rides from the east, he rides to the west through the path of
the sun

Riding without a saddle, riding with no stirrups
It is a horse of poetry he is riding, riding-riding
Here he comes riding with peace and authority this is the horse
of poetry
He rides into Spain, into England, riding up into crowded Beijing
Straight and bold he rides into Jerusalem
The ass of poetry he is pressing up and down
It screams like a donkey, it starts like an African zebra.
For how long will he ride the poetry pony?
Because it is now time he should rest
It is not a horse that he could dismount; it is not – the horse of
poetry
There are many journeys still for him to accomplish
In his capacity to ride the horse of poetry
It does not complain, it does not easily tire, it does not – the
horse of poetry
It is remote controlled, it is politically vulnerable
But he continues to ride, ride and riding; riding away the horse of
poetry
It flies in the deserts; it fords across crocodile infested rivers
It has no boundaries it has no limits it is a horse of African
poetry
He is riding, never coming back to the stables
Riding up riding down, riding up and down
He rides like a Ndebele, riding good; he rides like a Russian;
riding hard
Against the wind he rides, he is riding against the high tide of the
sea
He is riding against the mountain slope.

She is boiling, she boils a poetry cauldron
It is afire, the poetry cauldron boiling on the hearth

Making an American poetry soup, the cauldron of poetry is
boiling
She is adding some firewood, she is stirring with a wooden ladle
It is a poetry soup that she is boiling, boiling and boiling
It is a recipe that has no measure, it is a great deal of poetry soup
It is simmering, it is sizzling she is boiling away the poetry
cauldron
For how long will she continue to boil it?
Because she has been boiling it for long now
And a voice said to her at last:
Take a chicken, don't cut it up; throw into cauldron
Take tomatoes, don't cut them up; throw into cauldron
Take a bottle of cooking oil, don't open it please; throw into
cauldron
Take a packet of salt, don't open it up; throw into the pot
Take some Royco soup, don't open it; throw into cauldron
Take onion, don't cut it up; throw into cauldron;
And the voice said to her again:
This is the poetry soup in the making
Boiling, sizzling; simmering away the soup of poetry
Boiling up boiling down boiling up and down
The fire is burning high the coals are burning low
She stirs with a wooden ladle, she stirs up and down
The poetry cauldron is boiling, it is boiling down
For how long will she continue boiling it?
The people's hunger will make them die.

He is loading, he fires a poetry musket
He fires in the morning, firing at point blank
It is a poetry musket that he fires
It barks, it chatters as it discharges
For how long will he continue pulling the trigger?
For how long the poetry musket spraying death flashes

He fires without caution he fires without discrimination
It is a poetry musket in the hands of a Zimbabwean soldier
It is a Zimbabwean poet, a soldier and a musket
He is a trained Officer firing the poetry musket
Aiming his shots now without hesitation
From a hidden position he is firing and firing
It is a poetry musket discharging high explosive tracer shells
He advances he attacks he defends in some dug-ins
With the poetry musket fitted with optical sights
He fires up he fires down, he fires up and down
Yet it is a war that he fights against a sneaking enemy.

Poetry Of Change
Killian Mwanaka

if i were a poet
i'd like to sing to the wind
talk to the birds
and dance to the rhythm
of the autumnal breeze

i'd like to write without punctuation
capitalscomasfullstops
they block my mind
I'd like to write question marks???

i'd like to tell my people
of a hijacked revolution
lies and hypocrisy
and tell the president (mugabe)
that 'enough is enough'

i'd like to tell my people
i'm one of the guerrillas
who fought with tears of steel
and sweat of blood
to liberate the cronies?

i'd like to tell the president
that the people need
foodsheltermedicineandemployment now
and not
liesdeceitcorruptionchicanerymurder
cressidasbenzandbmws
shitting monoxide

if i were a poet
how can I write of beautiful flowers
of the rolling landscape
how can I
when people perish in this heavenhell on earth
where survival of the most cunning
is the order of the day
where mugabe and his cronies
belch like maggots in a frothy latrine
where harare stinks the stench of mukuvisi*

if i were a poet
i'd like to write
Poetry Of Change

*mukuvisi – a small dirty and polluted river that dissect and runs west of
Harare

Dear commissar
Mbizo Chirasha

dear commissar
my poetry is
political baboons puffing wind of vendetta
splashes of sweet flowing buttock valleys of pay less city
labourers
rough crackling red clay of sanctions smashing poverty corrupted
face of my village
presidential t-shirt tearing across bellies of street hustlers
mute bitter laughter of political forests after the falling of political
lemon trees

dear commissar

my poetry is
foot signatures of struggle mothers and green horns
bewitched by one party state cocaine
new slogan hustlers boozing promises after herbal tea of change
rhetoric
street nostrils dripping stink and garbage
tears chiselling rocky breasts of mothers who lost wombs
in the charcoal of recount

dear commissar
my poetry is
rhythm of peasant drums dancing the new gimmick
unknowingly
political jugglers eating voter drumsticks after another ballot loot.

POETRY
Elizabeth Semende

Poetry is perhaps the mouthpiece of a voiceless heart.
Poetry is perhaps the eye balls of a blinded soul.
Poetry is everything;
Poetry is everyone.

A remedy to the youths of a paralysed nation,
Hope for a people mired between the walls of a broken paradise,
Poetry is the song carried by the wind to the ears of every broken
heart,
A river overflowing with sublimity and grandeur.

Poetry is the dream I see when my eyes are closed.
Poetry is the ecstasy of words 'tween the pages of my journal.
Poetry is a shrill voice when the world is asleep.
Poetry is bliss, its presence a solace.

Poetry is the trigger of a gun with no bullets;
Poetry is safe.
Remove a word, withdraw a comma;
Perhaps it transfigures,
But the meaning lies in the heart of the beholder.
Poetry is a mystery.
Poetry is magic.

Poetry is the evolution of a love unexampled.
Poetry is the revolution of the mind.
Poetry is equality,
A change craved by the bone of the soul.
Poetry is a haven, nursing the emotions of a dark soul.

Poetry is me,
Poetry is you!

My Heart Cries
Lovers Pamire

Though l smile
Though l converse
Though l do daily chores
My heart bleeds
My heart cries down beneath

My heart cries
Crying for dreams shuttered.
Crying for ambitions strangled,
Crying for stolen love,
Perceived endless love
Cries for aborted future
Unchartered future, gloomy and so bright
The adage goes,
'Love is an attraction of the opposite',
Opposite of the heart

The tears are concealed
As in pregnancy
The inside is unseen
But visible at a close vista

The ink and the pen
Are messengers of the heart,
Connected intimately to deliver
The heart's cry on paper.

My Foot
Learnmore Edwin Zvada

Perhaps not my overzealous foot
I cannot take you on my date tonight
You continue to add injury to my amorous impediment
I have gone from date to date
Walking this path with you
You are slow at your step
Every time we set out to hunt for 'the one'
You linger to caress those shapely pebbles by the brook
I cannot trust you to let me go once you are tamed
The waters of the river lie in wait
For that day you take me into the April sunset
I cannot discern the color you are
You go from feisty to dull
From glum to twinkle
Someday you're heavy at my standing
To bend me over when you are too lazy to heave
In a near moment you could fashion another disturbing gait
Wobbling under the scrutiny of a potential mistress
Stay this expedition my foot
Perhaps and another day as I implore

Ndabaikana!
Shadreck Matindike

Chakandibaya chinenge chakatyokera nhaka,
Dei chisina chaisvotoka nekutumburwa!
Wakandiroya anenge akafa,
Dei arimupenyu airoyonora ahwatsitsi!
Chandakanwa chidhaki,
Dei arimaheu dzungu raienda!

Kukurukura hunge wapotswa, pakavandurirwa!
Ini ndobwereketa handina kupotsewa!
Ndiye mutsikapanotinhira, Lisa mwana akanaka!
Nemiseve yerunako rwake akandibayapamoyo, ndabaiwa!
Ndiye zidenderedzwa zai rehanga, ndatenderedzwa musoro!

Ndodii hangu neyangu nhamo?
Ndangariro dzongomhanya segonzo rawira muchirongo
chisinamvura!
Zvawandibayamoyo, Ko izvozvi ropotsozvewangu muromo
hazvina kutesvera here?
Zvandava hangu yekugochanyama, wadii waitabayawabaya?
Ndabaikana!

She Tickled my Fancy!
Interpretation by Shadreck Matindike

What I am feeling is not a dream,
If it was a dream I would wake up!
The one who bewitched me is dead,
If alive my case would be reversed out of empathy!
What I drunk is fermented,
If it was maheu, I would be sober by now!

He who escaped trouble lives to tell it all, they lied!
Am telling it all, I am busy in the trap!
Am in a hormonal civil war, my mind in seventh heaven!
What can I do? She drove me to cupid and back, her back!
Her back legacy, like lump of disturbed jelly move delicately!
My eyes are blessed with glimpses of glitters, all day long!

An angel personified she is, her voice is angelic!
Her beauty is packaged in sympathy and empathy, she is
beautiful!
With the push of love she pushed me, I am fallen in love!
Her body is generous, it feeds my two babies!
Her ways are good, she taught my children the way to go!

What else can I do?
I will enjoy while the stock of my days last,
From own cistern I will drink!
How I fancy my wife, Media!
She tickled my fancy!

17

All in good time
Lisa Jaison

One day I will give you what you want
I will sink my claws and teeth deep into you and never let go
Ravage you with my love till you beg for mercy
That day there will be no mercy

It's the day I will tire of saying no
Then I will indulge you to the point of euphoria
Dig deep into your juices and suck you dry till you pass out
Leaving you delirious and gasping for more

Keep it up, you will get what you are asking for
I will cocoon you in my web and embrace you so tight till your
breath is shallow
Only letting you up for air to prolong my devastation on your
being
Making you a lifetime prisoner of my love

I am warning you. It will be intense, brutal and relentless
Unforgiving like the desert sun
The idea of escaping from it, a dreaded mirage
A sweet cancer eating away at your persona

You keep asking for just a little, a chance, a taste or a sample
I will give you a hard and addictive tinytiny bit
There will be no rehab for this loving, no AA, or narcotics
anonymous,
Any withdrawal will make you suicidal and hooked

It will be the day you walk into slavery, and become a convict of
your desires
You will lose yourself in me and I in you
Then you will understand the need to be careful what you wish
for,
Hush now, quit pestering, all in good time.

Buried Dreams
Constance van Niekerk

It was so long ago
But I remember it like yesterday
Every blow a scar
Forever imprinted on my heart
A reminder of self-betrayal
And how I let it down
Oh yes,
My heart
A cemetery of buried dreams
Aborted in their first trimester
Never to see the light of day
Bellowing from the depths of the dust
My heart
Haunted by the ghost of whom I once was
A face familiar yet so strange
Full of confidence, self-love and adventure
Bubbly and bouncing
The garments of my former self
My heart
scarred
broken still
Yet,
It was so long ago.

When The Lights Went Out
Troy da Costa

She set the fire in the back garden of our rundown two roomed
semi
It glowed and crackled and cast its light dancing in the darkness
And she glowed
More beautiful than I'd ever seen
As she poked and prodded at the embers singing me to sleep
And I drifted with the smoke and ash into slumber,
Because tonight the only thing she'll serve is a dream

A JOURNEY
Tavonga Maipe

Love is a journey
In which two lives walk
Hand in hand
With smiles, bliss and happiness
Carpeting their way

Love is a sweet journey
Whose road is shined by
Low perpetual glows of fire
Adorning the two souls of the two travellers.
With two hearts
Embellished by trust and faithfulness.

Love is a discovery journey
During which he gives you a piece of your soul,
That you never knew was missing.
It is a journey
During which you find yourself in him
And him in you.
It's a peregrination
During which you find someone
To hang around with, through your lifetime.
And you are ready to plant
Seeds of happiness, together.
And water them with trust and faithfulness
And eventually eat from the tree of love
That is never exhausted.

Love is a healing journey
That eases all the discomforts of the soul.

And heals every wound of the heart.
And cures every disease of the mind.
Healing the one who gives and the one who receives it.

Love is a journey
Where everyone becomes a poet
Where friendship is set to music
It's a journey
That needs to be travelled by two mad people.

The journey of love
Is like a war;
Easy to begin, but hard to stop.
It is one journey whose destination
We never want to reach.
It is a lifetime romance

I watched the rose wilt and die.
Thamsanqa Wuna

I was in the audience of my own character
Witnessing myself fall for you,
Irrevocable love it was,
A beautiful rose about to bloom.
I saw as I felt the emotions,
As butterflies fluttered in my belly,
The Goosebumps erupted on my skin,
As the fire ignited my body.
The touch of your hand made me shiver,
The slide of your finger made me weak,
Being with you woke my senses,
Our rose of love began to bloom.

I reminisce the joy we shared,
And the smile you etched on my face,
The laugh you forced from my mouth,
The tears you wiped from mine eye.
Never was there a dull moment,
Your charm brightened my day,
You brought light to my darkness,
You saved me in every way.
So in love was I with you,
And so were you with me.
Or were you?
But it was clear for all to see,
Our Rose was perfect.
And our love was worth it.

But winter came, alas.

And froze our rose to bits,
I watched it whither and wilt,
I watched it bit by bit.
He came he saw and conquered,
And thus was my loss,
It's a burden I'll carry,
It is my personal cross.
And now I have accepted,
Our Rose has ceased to be,
You're to him his all,
But you were more to me,
It's sad to say, sad to know,
But no tear shall I cry,
I watched the rose bloom and grow,
And I watched it wilt and die.

Your absence puts me in another world
Hosea Tokwe

Lasting impressions, of kisses, a past record
The ever-love-illuminated soul bathes in darkness
A shadow of grief and solitude shudders the head
Whispers of glory and solicitude turn
Into ghostly echoes of bitter remembrance
Yet the attentive ear gasps for them
While the intrinsic eye draws for figures
Superlatively appetizing and tantalizing
But all is absolute vanity
Truly, your absence puts me in another world

A SMILE FOR THINGS TO COME STOOD TALL
Cosmas Shoko

I now know you are not mine,
In the haven of this heart you once lived,
Love flew beyond images an artist's paints,
Yet you were gone within a flash,
Woman, the echoes of your voice rang smooth in my heart,
My heart cherished your beauty,
All I know now, we were never destined to rise.

In the haven of this heart you once lived,
Woman, the day you walked bold with confidence,
The time to walk a new journey was alive;
A smile for things to come stood tall,
For seasons verily come to pass.

A new love freely touched this heart,
A sweet love to move beyond tests of time,
For she is a precious heart to adore and love,
The lady of my being,
Like daises she bloom so fine,
In her arms the heart sings a lullaby.

How much you mean to me
Hosea Tokwe

I have loved in the past, perhaps once too often
But all that's behind me now and should be forgotten
Speak of love's pains; I've been through them all
Some have been great and others small
I've given much love, inspired great hope
But the heartbreaks I've had were just too much to cope
I withdrew into a protective shell
So that no-one would be able to tell,
That I've been through it all, HELL UPON HELL!
My heart was so hardened, I seldom forgave,
People would call me a dumb arrant knave
Then you came along
As graceful as a swan,
I knew right away that you were the one
For whom I'd been waiting and would truly belong to
Your beautiful face, your enlightening smile,
Your maidenly grace and voluptuous profile,
Were all taken in, in such a short while
I've never believed in love at first sight.
But experiencing it all sure gave me a fright.
I cannot forget the day we first met,
Ever since then there's been no regret.
Time spent with you erases all memories of grieving
I certainly hope it's not the past I am relieving
For you are a candle lighting my way,
Turning all darkness into the brightness of day
All memories of you I'll always retain
And in your company is where I wish to remain
For you are a source of inspiration, my true love's pride

With you by my side I could easily ride
The trails of life and torn out the tide
I long to see the radiating glow enhancing your face
To feel the warmth of your loving embrace
And hear the sounds of your joyous laughter
This shall ring in my ears for time ever after
The beginning of new life is signified by spring
With the beautiful flowers blooming
And the jacaranda's blossoming
But such beauty of nature is only a temporary thing,
For what can be seen only lasts for a while
But what cannot be seen will last forever
Nature will lose its beauty with the coming of autumn
But my love for you will still flourish and won't need a post-mortem
For love is a spiritual gift, invisible to us all
It cannot be touched, smelt or tested.

Do not blame the Mirror
Albert Nyathi

Everybody is watching you
Watching yourself in the mirror,
Feeling important,
Feeling indispensable,
Trying to remove those spots
In your face,
The speck in your eye,
Hoping no one else is watching you
Watching yourself in the mirror.
Do not be angry with the mirror,
Do not smash the mirror,
The mirror is not to blame,
The mirror is only a messenger
Showing you who exactly you are.

Ego Protector
Lisa Jaison

I don't know when I became such a phony liar, liar with pants on
fire
I emerge as a fraudster driven by fear and conformity
Possessing an irrational desire to be liked and accepted by all
Either way herein lies a concealed me
A malicious ego protector at the expense of truth

I scam mercilessly when I pronounce your performance worth
while
Deep down I am annoyed at how you got yours and gave up
before I got mine
I know that this your performance is a dismal rendition and I
have had better,
But still I smile sweetly and fib dangerously
Claiming it's well and that I have reached dizzying heights
When deep in my core I marvel at what a wretched waste of a
minute it has been
While all the while I look you in the eye and stroke an ego that
serves me no good

My nose should just get elongated forever like Pinocchio's
Letting you down gently even though you are trying to murder
me with boredom with all your sweet intrusive nothings
I ponder if it is humanly possible to be that shallow, course and
crass
I am certain nobody wants to be so savagely, and relentlessly
pursued by a near stranger
In the real world, they call this creepy thing you do stalking,

31

Meanwhile I stand here afraid to smash and bruise that glass
house that is your ego
Placing myself in danger when I should scream bloody murder,
run for the hills and have you confined

It's blasphemous to silently walk away amid a blast of cat calls
In a ceteris paribus a brick in each mouth that dared it would
suffice for that sort of objectification
Surely, behaving like less than, should actually make you less
than.
We both know you do not have the spine to step to me without
the back up of your groupies
Perhaps my lying, fearful silence excuses this, make me a truth-
sayer so I can speak my heart
Allow me to call the zoo.
We both know baboon calling is for primates and you are best
joining your lot

Some days a shameless hypocrite stares back at me in the mirror
Feeling a false sense of security when they tell me she deserved
what she got because she was not full of decorum like me.
 I concur with this knowing full well she could be me, I am
complicit in denouncing her being and morals
Just grateful for my safety, your acceptance and the false sense of
sanctuary
I let you define her fate by confining her to your ideal, while
being complicit in defining my fate too
Staring back in the mirror at the one who caresses your ego
I won't utter that nonsense, no one cares that how we treat
people is a reflection of who we are and not who they are
Oh! The irony, with this person in the mirror

Deceit is incomplete without the manipulation

Planting little great ideas in your mind that I want you to
germinate
So that when that eureka moment hits you, we can all marvel at
your wisdom
Dimming my light to let yours shine brighter, because I really
have no inkling to intimidate you with my smarts.
Lest you with-hold the ring and the title that comes with it at all,
Instead, I wizzle and fib to get this that I think I need
Accepting the lie that I am nothing without you
I stoop to the bottom to get that which is worth more than my
integrity

Don't judge me, we all know the truth is overrated
Telling it as it is, is for angry people, they are unfamiliar, not real
and have a chip on their shoulder
Understand, it is an absolute lie, the truth will not set you free!
let those truth-telling misfits deal with their own holier than thou
conscience
Who cares about a sense of self when you could get blissfully lost
in this web of mendacities?

Be like that author who wrote about the truth being an unclear
path in the desert
After all the truth is relative so I lie the lies I need to lie,
The world should show me some gratitude, it's a nasty job, and I
have perfected the art of doing it

Don't look at me oddly when I insist I am fine
You know its untrue, I know its untrue but who cares for the
truth
I have held back from expressing what I really feel for so long
that these lies have become my truth

No one likes a vocal and outspoken damme and I am not going to displease you by being that in the name of truth
Feeding your ego is better than the high road, you have become my high road
So don't look at me askew as I stroke your ego,
I promise I am fine

to tolerate your petty insecurities
To stroke your ego and tell you that I do not notice the mature males oozing haves

THE GUILTY TRIP
Tendai Rinos Mwanaka

It's a careen, careening into the trail, every time we have arguments. It's always, I didn't show her that I love her well, better, good (which is not well), and best…I don't know which one here. It's getting such that I feel I am upended between the hard place and a rock. That little space changing me, the way neighborhoods changes us, for the worse. I want to love her the way she wants me to do it- but I want to love her the way I know how. Days when she rapes me for not loving her, it's like I have squashed a bug by accident. It was on its trail, rail trails on my body, and I thought it was a dangerous and poisonous thing or a pest, like lice. I must now repent. She persecutes me, I feel I must repent to her love, to her sensitivity, to her woman, and I am left with so much guilty, careening on a guilty trip, trail. Is my love a form of misuse? Not a site for her. I am forced to keep asking for my scales back, my animal form. I know it is always good to think through before exploding, to cut out your darlings, but someday I will tell her off. I would have to risk out swimming inside her heaven
I will say the Erin Moure(s) to her (telling off her vampire cling, the need to cling and cling in her).

"Listen, Parrot, I know you are hungry (a hungry sucker for love); *and that you don't like yourself. I know you sometimes fly."*
"I am not a parrot. I would rather you had said I am a pigeon or the proverbial sheep in the bible," she would refuse this naming. She is a bloody fighter.
"Get a life!"
"What?"

"Change! Shift, shape up, be say, a dove (not the pigeon she wanted
me to name her) *or sparrow, a weedy plant, a furious imprecation, a
ghost."*
"Really!"
Her whinnying is getting on my nerves

It doesn't bother me if she changes into a ghost and climb on top
of me, on my body, to receive seeding. Then I will gloss, guilty
free, my cornucopian perishables here, have a roasted cob!

Mount Hampden
Patricia D. Dube

Take me with you in my neon bib I am a hustler,
Mbare, Cuppa Cubana, I am a *riddim* king;
take me in my micro mini and find me a spot
under a new fluorescent street light
Take me to Mount Hampden
 I'll pretend to clean your shiny Ranger,
 in exchange for a cheap meal

TO MY MOTHER-IN-LAW

Robson Isaac Shoes Lambada

Wherefore then have you
Brought her out of your womb
That she had given up the ghost
And no eye had seen her
She should have been as though
She has not been
Better if she had been slow-marched
From the womb to the grave
She utters vain knowledge
And fills her belly with the east wind
Reasoning with unprofitable talk
She dines with stupidus and folly
Drinking iniquity like new wine
She takes the sheaf from the hungry
Eating of the basket of the don't-haves
Should she not be cut off
As the tops of the ears of corn

She toys with my heart
Counterfeiting passion at my sight,
Arching rhythmically her back
Like an oversexed peacock
Her body with me,
Her heart without
Lascivious to strangers in my court
She is a sister to dogs
And a mom to owls

With her tongue blessing

With the same my image cursing
As she darts her folly like a serpent's tongue
It is accounted to her for vanity
Wherefore then have you
Brought her out of the womb
Oooh!
That she had given up the ghost
And no eye had beheld her
Profitable if she had been carried
From the womb to the pit

LAMENTATIONS
Nellah Nonkondlo Mtanenhlabathi

How do I even call you a brother?
A brother who steals her sistren's minerals without mining rights,
A poacher trespassing
Eager to hunt for an innocent cub in a prohibited area.
Tell me, why degrade a fertile realm?
Tell me, why deplete another man's territory?
Tell me, will you replenish it?

A decade of existence and already you are decrypting an
encrypted code.
Am I not supposed to unlock my own door when I want?
Am I not?

You my brother is a renowned hero,
A protagonist
One famous for pulling down undies
One with courage to force his humongous tail in a tiny hole
One who never felt culpable for despoiling his blood.
Tell me, how am I supposed to sit and dine with you?
Tell me, how will I ever repeatedly shout your name?

What kind of a being breaths without conscience?
This was never a Beauty and the Beast episode.
Pray never to have a son
For my wreak will be your terminus!

Broken Future
Jurgen Martin Namupira

There she is,
Look at her.
She sits there;
Only those few moments has stolen to rest,
But her mind in sorrow,
Contemplating on who she would have been in life
Her Future destroyed;
By those who gave her life,
They could've sent her to college
But they sent her to marriage
Regret;
A pain in her heart,
A memory she can't escape,
Caught up in this trap.
Her dignity is lost;
To some man of the past,
Forced on her,
And they say it's tradition
Little girl wonders;
"My peers are in uniforms;
Holding pen learning to become nurses,"
While she holds broom learning to be a wife.
She is the same girl;
Who could've been the great lawyer,
But rather turned into a breeder,
The girl of a Broken Future.

Bars
Constance van Niekerk

She awoke with a fright.
Deafening screams,
Body violently shaking,
Drenched in sweat,
blood and fear.
Cold un-feeling steel
restraining her hands.
Was it a nightmare?
Or her mind bringing
to remembrance,
a cold deed long done.
She scanned the
unfamiliar surroundings
Dark, with a pungent odour
narrow bed, bare and stiff
Puzzlement and confusion
Clouded her mind
Was it just a nightmare
or was she paying for a
dark deed long done.

Resilience
Albert Nyathi

We are malleable,
So when you push us we fall,
But we fail to break
We are slippery, we are jelly,
We have our way,
You bend us anyhow
We never break,
Not even our spirit
You burn us, but the ashes rise again
We are your eyesore.

We are a fresh wound
Refusing to heal,
So we will never be a scar
Blood oozes all the time
But we never die
We drink the cool drink
Of our sweat.

untitled
Cosmas Shoko

the wheel of life,
to see a new ideal, live
with a heart of hope.

NKUNKUMINA YABINGA

Aleck Nchite Munkuli

Cde Andrew Sikajaya "Bigman" Muntanga

Bwakalibuzubabwa 20 gandapatimumwakawa 1937
Nkunkuminaniyazyalwa
WakatambulwaaabantubaMulwizikuntshelelaMuukase
Tebakazizipe, bakamuliikazinalya Syakajaya
Izinalyakalyambwida, wakazulwidachisi cha Binga
Bulilemekedwebulabwakanyampulankunkumina
Waakimikilakumajwiaakwe
MpawoBingayakasumpuka

Wakimininabantuluundumbuluzulwa
Wakalamalotombulimuntuwoonse
Amulangewakalotelachisimbuchizulwa
Wakakakakutimalotoakweabekabuyole
Wakalyabakutimalotoakweataswekipesiazwidilile
Wakiimachimpayumakunemboankondo
AwowalikuzulwidalwangunukolwamuTonga

Balikutwiitakutitulibanyama, tulibabi
Nkekakobalikutituyeeyambulibanyama
Tulamichila, tulatunwetotatwe
Bakalibalipakuti Zambezi ngwaabo
Balikulyabilabuvubibwesumbulimbubayanda
Balikumulangilaaaansitegwatayiide
Nikubabobotakachebukamusule
Wakinkililakunemboakwambasimpe
Mandongomutolakubushonaluzutu
1980kutongakwasimwami pharaoh kwakamana
Kwanjilabapati"Bigman"muPalamende

44

Kwakalibonyalumwemwelusikakumakosi

Lino twabukatobaTonga
Bwachaakulindiswe
Zubalyazwidamwiamatwikampoto

Bakasitedipalupalupalumulizyanyika
Bakasikulangileaansi
Nibakabonabanikenikebayiide
Balubakutibbwalolyakawumyamukamulombe,
Mukamunenekaseka.
1995 lyakulyalubopande
KuPalamendetensibalikubuzya
Bakalizikutitodinkilwinsete

Tachikwekubwedamusule
Malotoakweakazuzikizigwa
WakangwapandelyabuMPlwachibili
Kwindilamukuketwamulumuunoaluundu
IjwilyabaTongalyakamvwikana
LwangunukolwabaTongaluyekubaTonga
TwakaziteyanswimuliZambezi
Twakagadamabbasi,
Zikoloamakkilinikazyakayakwa
Twakachaansipabachinkondya
Wakazulwidamuluyandolwaluundulwabinga
KaswiniBamabulongobwangubwamana
Nkechilimuchisimu
Ndabulajambawisimombe.

Aamenamuchilataababi,
Kufwakwakokwakatujumaakabamaanziatikaaatakwebuyoleke
Bulyankuyubulinzizyania

45

Chikedendibbwe
BaMuntanga, simulizyangomatalikambili
Lekatukudundizyemwanabulongo
Silwizimupati, Muuyawakoulaleakupumulamulumuuno.

THE LION OF BINGA
Translation by Aleck Munkuli

For Cde Andrew Sikajaya "Bigman" Muntanga

It was on 22 in the month of October 1937,
An iconic leader and a hero was born
Accepted and acknowledged by the village of Basilwizi
They didn't know, yet they named him Siakajaya
The bonfire of the people's revolution.
The voice of liberation.

Blessed is the womb that carried the hero
He stood his ground and by his words,
And BINGA was lifted higher
He stood for the people
He had dreams like any other men
But, look he dreamed for the people of Binga
He could not allow his dream to flop
He surrendered his life to achieve his dream
He tirelessly fought forward
In all this he was putting a black person first.

They had labelled us, we are black
Therefore our minds and brains are black,
They had guaranteed,
The land and the Zambezi river was theirs,
They took the lion's share, shared the goodies amongst
themselves
They turned and played around with us
They didn't want objections from us
He tirelessly fought forward

In all this he was putting a black person first.
1980, the chains of King Pharaoh were broken
The sun rose up in Binga
He gave a slight smile
No more turning back!

This dream should be fulfilled.
He became the Member of Parliament in Binga
They looked down upon you
Not knowing that old people have tricks
They use to trick the boss.
1995 back in the parliament under the people's calling

Things changed
People's freedom, be to people,
He led under people's calling
Not forgetting that, "Umuntu ngumuntu ngabantu"
Never and Never ever shall we be colonized again
This dream should be fulfilled.
Every face was smiling country wide
Schools and clinics were built.
The constitution was implemented in our favour
The rights were right in our hands,
You were a dedicated man
Because of your good work

The death robbed us of an icon
Comrade Muntanga, your foot prints remain our inspiration.
Your life remains our Beacon of hope.
Let's follow his footsteps
Let's not trample his efforts to do our will
Let's hold on, in his words, "Munhu munhu nevanhu"
Son of the great river, May your Soul Rest In Peace.

TODAY IS THEIR DAY (HEROES' DAY)
Edward Dzonze

Stone upon stone,
Our lovely house is built; The House of Stone
There, within the Great Zimbabwe enclosure
A story is carved in blood and tears on every patch of ground
A story that bore us this freedom
A story with some chapters
Befittingly captured at the Heroes' Acre
Where enshrined memories are as sour as salted lemon
Yet from those sour memories, the freedom flower is rooted
Hooray to freedom, today is their day
Do you remember Cde
When we used to dream of freedom from the cold embrace of
servitude in colonial manacles
The Chimurenga songs we sang
Being the only melody that kept the dream in sight?
Proclaiming our loyalty to the cause through rhythm and rhymes
Taking our lives to the extreme edges of survival
Of what use is life without the privilege of freedom?
I know of men and women
Who stood in the way of a fired bullet
With a mere bow and arrow; black pride their shield
Standing firm and resolute in defiance of oppression
Freedom fighters; heroes of the land
Men who broke the colonial cage
To write the freedom story on an African page

Today is their day;
Men and women of valour

Whose names I can't spell on a poetry page
Men who traced the strength of Nehoreka
To find it lingering embedded in the blackness of their being
Women who found a melody in Nehanda's prophecy
And yielded to the bloody dance of Chimurenga chiming bells
In gunshots and detonating bombs
Men and women who dared the jungle bare footed
Putting out a ferocious flame with their own blood
Among them boys
Who, instead of dancing to the irresistible melodies
Of Jerusarema in the African villages
Took after their fathers in chasing the oppressor from the turf
Men and women who tasted vile
To serve this freedom so sweet
I can't resist to share the taste in poetry verses
Among them girls
Who took their chastity to the battlefield
To labor with fellow Cdes the birth of this freedom hard won
Men and women who walked the narrow of life
Fighting a system that gave us boundaries in our own town
Cde Tongo was among them,
Men who rose beyond heights for a human cause; Heroes

Hooray to freedom
As we sing Simudzai Mureza weZimbabwe
Today is their day, lest we forget the heroes of the land
Who pledged to their dear lives
To ignite the fight for freedom,
Who served jail terms
In restoration of national pride and dignity
Men and women of valor, freedom fighters
Who tended to the national call
In vigil of the sacrosanct walls; Masvingo eDzimbabwe

Upon which they were to hoist the freedom flag
Men and women massacred at Chimoio and Nyadzonia
Whose strewed blood watered the freedom flower to blossom
Men who rose above fear
To become themselves the currency of what the nation wanted
I know of some, whose bones are highly honored at the Heroes'
Acre
I know of some, who saw the entrance to the battlefield
But never the exit even when the battle was won
I know of some, who are still nursing
The wounds they sustained in battle
How can we forget,
We see their faces and worth on the colors of the national flag
We sing them everyday in that sacred hymn;
Simudzai Mureza wedu weZimbabwe
How can we forget, again I ask
They lived a purposeful life
That casted an everlasting shadow upon the land
They taught us to rise above fear
And today I sing their names with pride
What they became out of what they believed; Heroes
Let the freedom flag wave peacefully upon The House of Stone-
That was their warring urge,
Their desired will and wish
We can only honor them that way
Today is their day, Heroes' Day

YOU WERE THERE
Chido J. Ndoro

You were there
When their rule came to a screeching halt,
As the chains were smashed
And the grip of repression let go.

You were there
When they were overpowered,
As your spirit merged with the bodies of your children,
And your strength combined
Released them from the grip of oppression.

You were there
When our mothers fasted all day
So we could eat,
As the whip of the master
Lashed on their backs in the field.

You were there
When our fathers left home
To fight,
As their blood flowed in the rivers.

You were there
When we were whispering
Of dissatisfaction
With the way of life,
The fear of being heard
Overpowering us,
Paranoid

For there was no one to trust.

You are here
As we look to the spirit,
Asking;
If we have the right to rest,
When you died years ago
Without tasting freedom,
Do we have the right to demand for freedom?

You are here
As we search for answers
To unasked questions.
We listen
To the ancient voices
That whisper in our dreams
Hoping to solve the riddles
That this suffering life throws at us.
You are here
As i wander in this world,
As i become one with the dust,
Stinging the eyes of your children,
Clinging on to their feet,
Asking;
Do you have the right to be free?

FORGIVE THEM NYONGOLO.

Nellah Nonkondlo Mtanenhlabathi

Hypocrites!
Daylight Pharisees and midnight Sadducees
Long gowns to mislead you as they pay their so called respect
Yet at night they dance before your eyeballs in their birthday suits
Caressing the honourable War Veterans
Tightly clinging to their AK47
Opening wide the gates of their graveyards
To play hide and seek with the bullets
Polishing the corners of their beautiful mountains with bullet cases

Your daughters, father!
Daughters of the soil,
Disgracing and humiliating themselves
Before your very presence!
They know what they are doing Tata
Only they know why they do it
Just forgive them Nyongolo.

They have betrayed you,
From the day you shepherded your father's herds
Till today before your metal bones.
They have traded your sons breath
For the bond notes they never worked for.
For the love of money like Judas Iscariot
They deceived you and sold your soul
Not once but twice!
Like Mkabayi they played cowards and stabbed you in the back.

They know you love your people
But they teach them evil ways that hurts you.
You saw them giving her *umuthi*
Which kissed your grandson's life goodbye
For the love of power they will do anything
They might even steal the new metal you,
Sell you to outsiders
Just to gain control over your family!

Teach them the good ways of making a living Tata
Send them to their forebears if reluctant
Yet, forgive those who plead for clemency

Murder Most Foul

Jabulani Mzinyathi

They are killing the pan African spirit
Forged in the many years of repression
The masses wallow in deep ignorance
Grasping the lessons in self-hate
Blind to the divide and rule tactics
That seem to have stood the test of time

The victims of colonial domination
The victims of foul stinking apartheid
Now locked against each other in deadly combat
Pointing accusing fingers at each other
The architects of poverty rub their hands in glee
While the victims feast on victims

While De Beers siphon away the diamonds
While Lonmin drinks black blood
Stashing the gold loot in London
While platinum, uranium and other minerals are stolen
The gullibility is plain to see
The fights over the crumbs are brutal

Poverty and crime a bustling industry
For the imperialist looters in our midst
The diversionary tactics are there
Yet our people are too blind to see
Fighting over the meaningless crumbs
Arise Africa arise get your sight now

AFRICA; TO WHOM IT MAY CONCERN

Edward Dzonze

Up and down the African streets in poetry verses
Dust is the majority, the gold is just a few
Purses are empty, prices are hefty
The haves are few, beggars are the majority
The cost of survival is forever going up
As I go further deep into deserted mine shafts
In search of a deserted fortune to keep up with the heights of fate
My sister's knickers drops down
As bread prices treble up
Selling her body to negotiate a meal for her impoverished family
The haves pay for it, not for the needy sister's sake
But for their own greed's sake

Beloved Africa
For how long shall you wear that gloomy face?
For how long shall you carry the poverty tag along with your
name?
For how long shall we feed the hungry children?
With mere stories to feed their empty bellies.
Stories-
Stories like once we had a spark before it turned this dark
Stories that never attempt to answer our only question;
For how long shall we live in this dark?

I refuse to lay low and spectate
While the radiance of my black skin
Is overshadowed by delusional trajectories sparked by greed
Beloved Africa,
You have got the land in plenty
I don't see how food prices are hefty

We've got dimples filled with gold upon our beautiful face
I don't understand how we are becoming a begging race
A blooming bosom of flora and fauna
There in the wilderness;
My fathers used to live in peace and harmony
Priceless curves that captures the eye with glitter
Bringing value to the body through its worth
I don't see how we are living poor with all the mineral wealth
We've got pendants of silver and copper
Dangled all over our body,
With the little drops of oil we have
Don't you think we can give the world-
A healthy smiling face?

To be this black and alive
His limitless grace paid the price
To be such without pride;
Is closing our eyes in pretence of blindness
Dear Africa; it is you whom it may concern
To conquer the darkness of days
All we need is a glow of light
Not the light from a fired bullet or a firefly
Rather we need lights in the African streets,
A light that sparks a sincere smile in every African home
A light that forever shines,
A light that shames darkness from our African homes
A light that illuminates the African spirituality
To awaken African pride in the conscience of all
A glow of light that shames corruption
A light that makes me visible,
A light that justifies our human worthy
A light that lasts the span of life…
To that end I proclaim my love for black.

Kaddafi
Mbizo Chirasha

I see America dancing in oil sodden nights, nostrils stinking the
scent of death
Your ghost exorcising demons of colonialist clout, walking along
banks of the lost river
River that lost its freedom
Your shadow suffocating under the smell of exile and scent of
slums
Kaddafi, propaganda is fart, fart deodorizing the winds of the
villages
I have a burning passion to bring back the dimples and wrinkles
of this country.

Am not black, but an African

Lovers Pamire

Is black or white a colour?

What is the nuance behind the two?

Is black the same as dark?
Is white the same as light?

Is black the same as bad?
Is white the same as good?

Is black the same as evil?
Is white the same as righteous?

Is black the same as ugly?
Is white the same as beauty?

Is black the same as primitive?
Is white the same as civilised?

Am an African, am I called black.
A black man, black in complexion
But, am l really Black?
I looked myself a million times in the mirror.
I could not transform into a black colour.

What is the meaning of black?
Can black be replaced by brown?
What is the meaning of white?
Can white be replaced by beige?

A black man is in Africa.
Africa is developing, a third world's planet.
A white man is in Europe.
Europe is developed, a first world's planet.

Did the Creator named us black or white?

What is the meaning of evolution?
What is the meaning of civilisation?

I would rather call myself AFRICAN,
Lest I am caught up in between colours.
I am an AFRICAN man,
Fearfully and wonderfully made

Black Oranges
Mbizo Chirasha

Xenophobia my son
i hear a murmur in the streets
a babble of adjoining markets
your conscience itching with guiltiness like
genital leprosy
your wide eyes are cups where tears
never fall
when they fall the storm wash down bullet drains
and garbage cities
come nomzano with your whisper to drown,
blood scent stinking the rainbow altar
darfur, petals of blood spreading ,
perfume of death choking slum nostrils
slums laden with acrid smell of mud and
debri smelling like fresh dung heaps
fear scrawling like lizards on Darfur skin
kibera, i see you scratching your mind like ragged linen
smelling the breath of slums and diesel fumes
the smoke puffing out through ghetto ruins is the fire dousing the
emblem of the state
belly of Zambezi ache with crocodile and fish
villages piled like heaps of potatoes against the flank
of eastern hills
farmlands dripping golden dripping dew
sunshine choking with vulgar mornings
dawns yawning with vendetta filled redemption songs
drums of freedom sounding fainter and fainter, blowing away in
the wind
when streets rub their sleep out of their eyes
villagers scratch painful living from the

infertile patches of sand on this earth whose lungs
heave with copper and veins bleeding gold
ghetto buttocks sit over poverty, kalinga-linga
corruption eating breakfast with ministers, kabulonga
with shrill cries of children breaking against city walls
shire river tonight your voice rustled dry, like the scratching of
old silk
Politicians grow everywhere like weeds
land of ngwazi, yesterday crocodiles breakfasted on flesh
owls and birds sang with designated protocol
ngwazi your cough drowned laughters and prayers
your breath silenced rivers and jungles
Mozambique
the belief and gift of my poetry
sweat wine poured to absent, long forgotten gods and goddesses
soft kiss spent on golden virgins before they aged into toothless
grannies
the rhythm of samora
heartbeat of chimurenga
drumbeat of chissano
today mornings blight in corruption
a social anorexia
Abuja guns eat you more than disease
I loved you before you absorbed poverty as sponge
soaking out water
before rats chewed your roof
before you conceived men with borrowed names and totems
ghost of abacha guzzling drums of blood and gallons of oil
wiwa chasing shadows of babangida past delta of treasures
Buganda cruelty is a natural weapon of a dictator
poor lives buried under rubbles of autocracy
pregnant mothers with eyes gouged out by bullets, pushing their
guts

back into their bellies
luanda
a roar of old trucks
a whine of motor cycles
a rumble of dead engines
America frying its fingers in oil pans of your kitchen
where Europe fry, America roast
Angola, if you cough, America catch a fever
angola quench my parched lungs with a spoon of oil
i see the naked thighs of your desert hills
Barotseland Setswana
a servant positioned with trust
American green bloomed your desert shrubs
your loyalty is sold to she who offers the next meal
Barotseland of seretse
Somalia
your lips burnt brown with exposure of rough diet
you are muffled voice, cursed and drowned into deep silence
the smell of aged incense and stale coffee
a tune piped by the shepherd on moutainside, only
to be half heard by and quickly forgotten by villagers
Ghana
the anthill of black seed
coast blessed with gold
once a young girl full of sap and strength
once perfumed with richness and sacredness
you shared your salt and sweat for freedom
today you are like a woman who sleep with a pillow
between her legs anticipating a miracle of man
coast of ivory
i see faces tight as skin of drum in moonlight
ivory coast, once the smoke and smell of human excitement
tonight bullet burrow into your belly like rats into sacks

64

of Thai rice
you are the broken pot we patch to put on shelf again.
flesh of children roasting in your belly, Darfur

The Woes of My Color
Debra Chimuka

Who has words to describe color?
Who has words to define man?
What meanest thou my skin?
Causing me woe and tears.

Alas thou art something to think about!
If you are so cruel
To take my sense of self
Who decides who qualifies for this color?
Who is the judge?

No one chose to be pitch black like baboons or
Pink like pigs.
Judging and criticizing;
And being judged and criticized
The chief root of separatism.

My color at the back of the class
This black unprivileged shade
Chained to my color, I change not
My skin cannot be from me nor can I.

There are no words to express
The feelings that overwhelm me when I am;
Degraded, patronized and profiled because of my color.
No! Don't touch me...

Anger and pain combined:
The pain shuts off the words
My breath gets shallow and heavy

The weight of pain is heavy
Resentment rocks my senses and body.

Without ways to fight back;
You cut me deeper than any knife could ever do.
I bled where you could not see
I bled within.

There was no blood but pain.
Your words and conduct cutting me into parts
Until there was no me…but only you.
Once you associate habits with color
Labels interfere with true identity.

My color is not a defect
A fair character the real meaning of a human being
That alone makes one superior.

My color is not stupidity;
Only my actions can be.
Beneath my skin
Is the key to finding me
Every color scheme is beautiful through;
Pure insight.

When one who is racially prejudiced dies or falls to the ground
Racial thoughts are buried with him.
The grave is closed;
Spite cannot touch me anymore.
This is my freedom and his bliss
As he lies resting in peace.

African Footprints
Constance van Niekerk

They cannot be found in sand.
There the wind will blow them away.
Cement is strong,
and will last long,
but hard to find after the storm.

They are marked in ink
that cannot be expunged.
They live in;
the sound of the rain,
the animals on the terrain,
the echoes in the mountains,
the mysterious caves hidden for ages,
the drum beats in the villages,
carrying ancient messages,
the stars shining like an enchanted blanket
covering the night sky,
the unforgettable sights,
the setting and rising sun on the horizon,
special moments on the beach,
the innumerable adventures in the jungle,
the gay laughter around the fire
and the endless jaunty chattering all around.

They cannot be found in the sand.
There the wind will blow them away.
They're left protected,
Jealously guarded
and ingrained in the hearts

of her people and all who pass her way.
They'll live a lifetime
They're her tracks,
Africa's footprints
In our hearts.

CHILDHOOD MEMORIES OF NYARUCHENA RIVER
Edward Dzonze

Somewhere in this Great Zimbabwe enclosure,
Somewhere in the lofty expanse of Kachepa village,
There among the granite rich mountains of Mutoko
There within the echo reach of Nyaruchena ripples
Beyond those mountains and plains
Far East of the capital city,
The flow of my blood
Drips from the sacred carvens of Chiparapara mountain
Wherein faces of my ancestry
Are painted on every dimple of mother nature
Sorry, I almost forgot
Even this tale here can be traced back to the same

Talk of Nyaruchena river,
So close to me, I could feel her heart beat at night
From my mud and pole cabin,
Ever serene through the peak of summertime down pour.
She enchanted me day and night
With her rhythmic flow
That formed the chorus of my childhood rural memories
Meandering through Katavhinya–Musanhi villages
I could capture the rise and fall of the tide
From the mean comfort of my puma blanket
If I can recall
I was 10, when I took my first dive
Into the river banks of Nyaruchena

We shared our nakedness
With girls older than us with no sexual intent
For all I knew;

We were told not to do the unthinkable
To avoid the wrath of the River gods
Or else Nyaruchena river would run dry
The River gods would swallow their water back- so we were told
Fifteen years then, at age ten
I lived by the book to buy myself the grace and favor of the River
gods
The river gods I wouldn't dare to imagine its looks
At least the river banks were not so tempting,
After all we were still learning to swim

With each dive
My love for Nyaruchena grew by day,
With each calculated dive
I learnt the tricks of the game,
Playing hide and seek
With the masters of the game
Was I not 13 or so
When I swam to the deep end of the pool?
The deep end where the masters swim
The very deep end, where the monsters feast
Yes I was only 13
When I left the lofty expanse of Kachepa village
There, within the echo reach of Nyaruchena ripples
I couldn't withstand dear Nyaruchena taking the nemesis of the
River gods in my face
I have never bothered to ask why and how
But news got to me;
Nyaruchena never ran dry
I knew then, it was a lie or better still a mystery-
Grownups don't lie in Africa
The River gods demystify with age

A Prize for the Black Eye
Hosea Tokwe

He pulled his oversized trousers
Sweeping through the dusty yard
Sides of his unwashed mouth frothing
Itching for a mug of the local brew
But none of the revelers paid him attention
So he staggered forwards backwards forwards backwards
Still his antics did not reward him
Thus when he cupped the sand and scooped it into Regu's mug
Up stood Regu in boiling anger
Like a possessed bull he advanced
Right…left…right…left combinations stung Chinyakata
The hard knuckles were driven into his cheeks hard and painful
They partially blinded him before he saw a glint of the last star
Leaving thick swellings on both cheeks
Black balls emerged that were painful to touch
He was silent, remained silent, his mouth gapping
But now his sober senses were returning
Yeah there sat the Headman, he could see
And yes Kerenge the comedian was there too
Kerenge with toothless gums he fought hard to suppress laughter
Chinyakata only blinked, as at last the mug got closer to him
A sure prize for his black eye

AIDS
Elizabeth Semende

When at dawn I tear off the curtains of shame
And divulge my wounds to the universe,
Though emotionally crippled,
I wish to break away.
Like sprouting plants on fertile grounds,
I want to break free from the cruelty of your eternal embrace.
But
No wind can blow you away,
No tomb can bury you under,
No ocean can swallow you within.
You remain among us.
You remain within my veins,
Building jails,
Forging tombs.
You confined me to a life sentence I cannot escape alive.
You killed me but spared my breath.
I'm dead today;
But still I breathe.

O, DEATH
It is among us you spread your limbs,
Pulling our tongues to lick the immortal wounds of our wailing
hearts.
O, Death,
Among the dead you are as dead as they are,
For silence lingers deep within you.
In darkness tombs lament from the heaviness of souls sowed
within.
O, Death,
You abduct smiles of yesterday

And merry, as we scatter bodies deep into the soil.
It is among us you strike cymbals followed by hymns of triumph, rejoicing,
as we, like a swarm of blind bees,
drown into pools,
besieged by your inviting snares.

O, Death,
Like whirlwinds you come and leave
after contaminating our memories
with sorrow.
Like petals of a budding rose you pluck friends and family into earth's womb.
But we shelter their ghosts deep within the dungeon of the soul.

THE STORM
Phumulani Chipandambira

when it rained blood
for a whole week
the sun went red
the bread
became stale
the citizens stayed put
the market stalls closed
hospitals opened not
no funerals
streets were deserted
even the milkmen did not turn up
no newspapers were sold
no news…..

it was a week not lived !

The setting sun
Jabulani Mzinyathi

The great fire ball
Riding majestically over all
Warming the waters of the lakes
Licking the mountain tops
The life wielding rays
Birds triggered to chirp
Mirthfully chirping in the trees
Expectantly waiting are the nestlings

Now the day is done
Disappearing behind the mountains
The foraging has now ended
That vivacity is now wished for
Reality delivers a thunderous back hander
Now at the end of the tether
Eagerly awaiting the rejuvenation

A Rural Woman
Lovers Pamire

Born out of the ordinary.
She wakes up before dawn.
Tiding and cleaning all chambers
That's the order of the day
She makes a fire from wooden logs,
Preparing children for school.

She tills the land for subsistence
When the moral is down and
Energy exhausted in the field,
She goes home and prepares food for all.
The sun is scourging
Bare footed she stumbles, but hard is the sore
Conditioned to the nature

Her beauty has faded away.
The sunrays have been merciless.
The smile is still notable, the nose and the ear still intact.
The eyes have turned crimson due to smoulder blowing,
But more still filled with love
Her voice a bit horse crying for the illusive breakthrough.

When the oxen are off the yoke,
She looks for greener pastures to fatten the cattle.
She battles with wobbly goats,
She dribbles past the snakes and maggots in the thick forest.
The day is fast fading away; children are on their way from
school.
She rushes home to prepare food for the entire clan.

She is the last to sleep and the first to wake up.

The sense of beauty is buried into the ancient times.
She sleeps like a log in the nights.
Her virtue is challenged by each dawn.
Shower is not a priority under the circumstances.
Manicure and pedicure is in oblivion.
Hairdo has been long since forgotten.

The life of a rural woman, un-equated talent,
An unsung heroine
When the summer is over, she makes apparels.
She sells clothes, meats and sundries.
She journeys on foot far and beyond.
She carries a stone luggage on head
For the upkeep of the family
Determination and motivation drives her.
Thus she keeps smiling through it all.
She never give up.

Mukadzi wekuna Zvirevo 31
Shadreck Matindike

Enda kuna Zvirevo 31, iwe mukadzi benzi!
Unzveree vakadzi vakachenjera maitiro,
Uzviwanire uchenjeri, usaupambadzezve!
Uhodhe zvokwadi, usaitengesazve!

Mukadzi wekuna Zvirevo 31 akanaka, anoita zvakanaka!
Anofadza wake murume, anofadza vese!
Haana ruoko nokuti haagariri maoko,
Haana remadunhurirwa zita rokuti "Baba-chakati-chapera",
Anotsvanzvadzira zvokudya kure nepedyo!

Haaiti zvengonono, Anova zikarunyanhiriri,
Anotarira vake vashandi mushando wavo,
Anoshereketa mumibato yake nenguva,
Anopunyaira, misodzi mizhinji kwaari,
Anonetera mumasango, zvipiwa zvevaneta zvizhinji kwaari,
Uyu mukadzi uyu anoputira mhuri nezvipfeko, chando
vanochihwira kumaraini,
Anotenga munda,nokuurima,
Akarimira napamuganhu nehope, haazezirima!
Uyu mukadzi haasimukadzi nhando,
Rurimi rwake gunorerauchenjeri,
Haabatikani muzvirehwa rehwa zvenhando!
Wake murume anokudzwa padare,
Vacheche vake vanoremekedzwa nokuda kwake,
Kwechiso kunaka handiko chete kwakanaka,
Kwemoyo kunaka ndiko kumwe!
Ndiye mukadzi anozvipfekera pasi pemurume wake chaiye,
anoremekedza murume!
Ndiye mukadzi anotya Mwari, dzakarurama dzake nzira!

Chaabata chinoendeka,
Waasangana naye anofara!

The Wife of Proverbs 31
Translation by Shadreck Matindike

Pass through Proverbs 31, ye foolish wives!
Consider the ways of the wise wives,
Wisdom you can acquire, don't sell it again!
Horde it, don't sell it again!

The wife of Proverbs 31 is virtuous, she acts virtuously!
For her husband she does good, she is good to all!
She does not have a hand because she does not sit on her hands!
Her nickname is not ' Honey, this has run out!'
Her eyes browse for food hither and thither!

She is not friend to snoring, she befriends the morning breeze,
On maidservants in their ways she mantains a close eye,
She keeps time, she always is on time every time!

This wife eats fruition of sweat, her quiver is always full!
Her household is clothed in Scarlet, it feels the cold in rumour
stories!
She buys her field and farm it, she cooks her cake and eat it!

This wife is not an ordinary wife!
Her tongue drips wisdom,
She is not a rumour monger!

At the gates her husband is praised, to his voice they listen!
Her offsprings are called blessed, she is a blessing to the
community!
Her beauty is not painted on skin, her beauty is within and
without?

The wife of Proverbs 31,
That's the wife after the heart of God, after the heart of her
husband!
Her nakedness is covered in principles, she knows how to cover
herself!
Her mouth is closed in wisdom, her silence is golden!
Her mouth is opened in wisdom, her speech is golden!

BEAUTIFUL WOMAN
Tavonga Maipe

As tender as her sweet voice
She is everything to everyone
She is a complete definition of life
Where there is no beautiful woman
There is an enormous void.

A beautiful woman
Swallows all the venom
Spitted by an aggressive man
And squeezes unconditional love
To the very aggressive man.

She calms the storms of every madness
And turns them to a sunshine of happiness
She creates heaven on earth
Where man dwells blissfully
And call it a world.

A beautiful woman
Is more beautiful than the mermaids of the sea
She is brighter than the stars of the sky
Her love is deeper than the waters of the ocean

A beautiful woman
Is not the one from America
But the one from God
She is not a sexy one
But a wise one.

They say

A beautiful woman
Makes a beautiful wife
But I say a beautiful woman
Makes a beautiful life
And eventually a beautiful world.

A beautiful woman
Is tender but strong
She gets hurt but forgives
She gets troubled but cares
She has little but still gives
A beautiful woman
Is never exhausted.

All what the world needs
Is a beautiful woman
She makes a beautiful life
And eventually a beautiful world.

THE MISSING PERSON
Phumulani Chipandambira

If you happen to see
a fagged woman
clad in ragged fatigues,
a frayed doek
and torn tennis shoes...

If you chance to see
a black woman
with a sorrowful face
and a soft voice,
please, remember to tell me.

She is my mother,
Lost in the city, looking for me.

Another day
Jabulani Mzinyathi

An epitome of countless tales
That is her sad song reverberating
A song of destitution and squalor
A song of parents long decimated
A grandmother eagerly waiting
Like a chick in anticipation in the nest

The likelihood of abuse looming
Roaming the unfriendly streets
The biting breeze she braves
Then she sings her solemn song
At times pocketing that elusive dollar
Another hectic day is now done

The Wretched Of The Earth
Killian Mwanaka

They live up there in Mt Pleasant
    and they live down there in Mbare Township

They live in posh houses
    and they live in the ghetto

They've never known hunger, they feast on five-course menus
    and they growl and crawl on empty bellies

They come to them dressed in fashion from Paris, London and
New York
    and they listen meekly, in tattered clothes and bare feet

They tell them of salvation they brought
    and they cheer and ululate

They tell them to give donations to be done for them
    and they give donations to be done for them

They tell them 'This is our culture'
    and occasionally mix, making sure their suits are not spoilt
And they do the real thing,
    chanting, clapping and dancing to the rhythm of
muchongoyo

They climb into their latest Mercedes Benz cars
    and they spatter the stony ground until feet crack.

*Mt Pleasant is a rich suburb in Harare
*Mbare is a very poor township in Harare
*Muchongoyo is a kind of dance played in eastern Zimbabwe.

ELECTIONEERING
Robson Isaac Shoes Lambada

Voting is the beginning of the ending of complaining
And abstaining id donating your right to choosing
My voice is a missile from the township crater
Dismantling the first regiment and commandos of your
politicized grey matter
Your voice is a bazooka from the side-lined population
Disintegrating the battalions of apathy and brigades of youth
marginalization
I choose to choose by voting
And choose laughing over fighting
Reasoning over sloganeering
And voting over toyi-toying
Voting is the beginning of the ending of complaining
And abstaining id donating your right to choosing

Annihilation'sedge
Patricia D. Dube

He had been walking on the edge of a sword
all his life, each deep cut to the sole reached
his soul, creating ever increasing crevices on his heart
He could not bear sharing, the darkness in his heart
but could only paint black portraits which
closely resembled the eclipse of his life
He lived on the edge of annihilation
gazing into the bleakness of paralyzing depression

CONFESSIONS OF A WAR VETERAN

Robson Isaac Shoes Lambada

Teach me the new slogan
I have already put down my gun
Though I drive the cancerous dictator's van
I will not give the new slogan a ban
I remain the revolutionary luminary's son

Dark clouds are below you
You now have dollar for two
How it all came to be true
I do not have a clue
Your sky is brilliantly blue
You now have dollar for two
How it all came to be true
I do not have a clue

Baker's Inn brown bread brilliantly baked and not burnt
All for dollar for two
Crusty creams chocolate coated crispy and curled by courteous
cookers
All for dollar for two
Street stylish straight stripped stockins
All for dollar for two
Ready to drinky, ripe and ready, fresh milk, your favourite fruity
fanta
All for dollar for two
Ten-packed, cancerous ciggareetes, tested and toasted
All for dollar for two
Pink pants for a poor partner, purposefully and professionally in
Peru butterfly printed

All for dollar for two
Shake-shake beer best brewed better than any brown beverage
All for dollar for two
Satisfying sufficient, not skimpy sex at Seke Growth Point
All for dollar for two

Never in my life did I hear of a for-two in Commerce
Never in my life did I hear of a for-two in Business
The only of a for –two I ever heard was in sickness
Two paracetamols twice a day
Two salbutamols for two patience in May
Sacharrine colcom curry pies all for
All for dollar for two
Women's once-worn underwears at Mupedzanhamo second-hand
wares
All for dollar for two

Tutor, Teach me the new slogan
I have already put down my gun
Though I drive the cancerous dictator's van
I will not give the new slogan a ban
I remain the revolutionary luminary's son

What Next?
Killian Mwanaka

After the gods became angry
And the sun disintegrated
Emitting arrows of fire

After the moon turned red
And the stars fragmented

After the heavens opened
And swords of steel clashed
And clouds rained blood
And vultures dropped balls of fire
Tearing apart pregnant mothers
And children, old men and women
And birds and baboons and lizards

After maize-fields
Turned into ashes
And mountains scotched barren
And humans imprinted with tattoos of fire

THE COCK CREW
Then there was metamorphoses
The birth of a CHILD

And after the Big Chiefs
Enthused in grandeur
The pinnacle of success
And basked in the sun
And talked politics and socialism

And structural adjustment programmes
And looted
And urinated on sacred rivers
And danced on graves
And vulgarised sacred places
And spat on old women's faces
And sipped whisky
And spewed spiralling smoke
And tore virgins
And drove limousines
And ate and died of obesity

And after children died of hunger and malnutrition
And beggars and street kids
Littered the streets of Harare

What next when men lost reason
And chaos reigned.

Uhleko lolu ngolwani?

Tembi Charles

Uhleko lolu ngolwani?
Zona izinto zimi mazonzo,
Uchago luyacitheka.
Kanti uhleko lolu ngolwani?

Siyahleka sigigideke.
Yona intaba idilika.
Isizwe siyatshabalala.
Kanti uhleko lolu ngolwani?

Bakwethu - vukani, qhaphelani!
Liyaduma liyedlula!

What is this laughter?
Translation by Tembi Charles

What is this laughter?
When things are in disarray?
When milk is spilling
What is this laughter?

We laugh, until our sides ache
Whilst the mountain is crumbling.
And the nation dissolves.
What is this laughter?

My people, wake up, beware!
Thundering rain is passing!

Gudo guru petamuswe

David W Mwanaka.

Pamakasvika sekuru takapemberera tikaita mabiko
Dzedu nyemwero nzeve nekunzva.
Tikati havano sekuru vedu vauya nemanyautsamukanwa.
Tikati sekuru vauya nerusununguko.
Vauya kuzosimudzira vazukuru.
Takaunganira sekuru kuti vatiudze nyaya dzinovakamusha.
Nyaya dzepasichigare nengano.
Nyaya dzerudo kuti isu vazukuru tiwanewo.
Nyaya dzekuti tese tisimukirewo tiite savo sekuru
Sekuru vakatimbundira neavomaoko mahombe.
Isu ndokutambarara tikati tadiwa nasekuru.
Tirizvedu pakati pemafaro sekuru ndokutanga
Kutisvina sehembe nyoro.
Kuti tichifema tatadza.
Tichiridzamhere ndopatoona shavi rasekuru
regudo kutipfacha kusvika.
Nechinguvachidiki homwe dzevazukuru dzose dzazunguzwa
ndokupera.
Inga sekuru votiita makwayi ivo vavegava.
Sekuru vaitanyoka yapinda muchikwere chine huku.
Sekuru votiangosimudza musoro ruoko pahuro.
Abvunza mubvunzo banga pamoyo.
Aonesesa maziso tuchu hanzi waonazvisizvako.
Achema nekurwadziva hanzi yatove mhandu.
Avadenha vodzorerwa kwamusikavanhu.
Zvino tavekuona kuti sekuru vakwegura vakabatauroyi.
Sekuru vedu wakachekerwa nyora dzekuba.
Iwo moyo wavo vakaora nechemukati.
Kuora semuti wapfukutwa moyo.
Ivo mahobi avo sekuru gudo akahwandisa umhondi.

Maziso avo anopenya rufu neutsinye
Kuita utsinye hwenyoka inoruma chaisingadye
Kuita hwenda inoruma akaitakura.
Kuzofarisa senhunzi yaone ndove.
Idzo nhafu dzavagudo dzekutotemerwa nyora.
Weduwe vedu sekuru umbimbindoga ndehwejongwe.
Jongwe rinoda kurira rega muchikwere
Maoko avo akazara ropa revazukuru
Iri ndiro riye shavi reruokorurefu.
Havaone kuti vakwegura.
Maziso adzoka mumahobi avo
Idzo njere dzapwa setsime muchirimo.
Sekuru vedu havazivi kuti vanengegudo.
Parinokwira mumuti gotsi rinengerakashama kumhandu
inemuseve
Havaone manyekenyeke emoto arikuuya
Ava ndivo sekuru vaye vatakagamuchira nemaoko ese
Imi sekuru kani.
Akurumanzveve ndewako.
Iyi iyambiro kubva kuvazukuru
Chisingaperi chinoshura.
Yenyu nhambemutambe regai ichanaka.
Chiregai zvekutamba nedhaka pasina mvura.
Vane ruzivo vakavayambira vakati.
Gudo guru peta muswe pwere dzigokuremekedza.

Old Baboon, fold your tail.
Translation by Tendai Rinos Mwanaka

When grandfather arrived we rejoiced and celebrated
With our smiles ears and listening.
We said here is our grandfather who has come with delicious
foods.
We said Grandfather has come with our freedoms.
He has come to uplift his grandchildren.
We surrounded grandfather
So he told us stories to build up families.
Stories from long ago and of fables.
Stories of love so that us grandchildren, we would find love.
Stories of success so that we could succeed like grandfather
Grandfather embraced us in his huge hands.
We became complacent saying, grandfather loves us.
When, in the middle of this happiness, grandfather started
To squeeze us like wet clothing.
Such that, to breath, we couldn't.
When we mourned loudly, we discovered the Baboon's spirit
Of our grandfather was to crash us before we arrived.
In no time our pockets were turned inside-outside, and emptied.
It seems grandfather has made us into sheep.
He was the wilddog.
He has become a snake in the hen's shelter, with the chicken
inside.
Grandfather killed everyone who raised his head.
Ask a question, and you are knifed at the heart.
See too much, eyes are gorged, for you saw what was not yours to
see.
Cry from the pain, you are an enemy.
Provoke him, and you are send back to the creator.
We now see that grandfather has witchcraft in ageing.

In our grandfather, it is cut into his skin the mark of corruption.
His heart is decaying in the insides.
Decaying like the tree, from the insides.
His deep forehead is like the baboon's, hiding cruelty.
In his eyes shines death and cruelty.
Like the snake's cruelty, biting what it doesn't eat.
Like the lice that bites its host.
He is too excited like a fly that has found a mound of cow dung.
His greedy is like the baboon's, a mark cut into the skin.
My, oh, my Grandfather's dictatorship, is like a cock's.
The cock that wants to hear only its crows in the hen's shelter
His hands are full of the blood of his grandchildren
This is the spirit of big hands.
He doesn't realize he is old.
Eyes have shriveled into his deep forehead.
His brain has dried, like a winter's pool.
Grandfather doesn't realize he is like a baboon.
When it climbs into the trees, its back is exposed to the enemies'
arrows
He doesn't see the ferocious flames of the fire coming
This is the grandfather we received with open arms
Grandfather, please! Anyone who advises you is your friend.
This is the warning from your grandchildren.
Anything that doesn't end is sacrilegious.
Your delicious food; stop eating it, whilst it is still tasty.
Don't play with soft clay where there is no water.
Those with wisdom have warned you, saying.
Old baboon fold your tail, so that little children would respect
you.

Predicament
Thamsanqa Wuna

I'm in a situation I never anticipated,
I feel helpless, hopeless and lost
This isn't the life I expected,
Misery, poverty and injustice for most
It's irrefutable we've been robbed by government,
They have left us all in the predicament
An abyss of internal screams and lost dreams,
Nothing compares to this pain I bear,
The burden I carry, the story I share.

The government has robbed this nation,
Turned the bread basket into a basket case,
They suppress our will at every election,
They preach lies and deceit to our face,
Of $15 billion, Zim-Asset and grandiose proposals
Of barred protests and responsibility refusals,
It's not up to politicians, but us citizens
To vote this dictator out of power,
And reclaim a heritage that's rightfully ours.

We need to be vigilant, we need to be true,
And turn out for polls in our millions,
It takes us; it takes me and you,
To fight for the future of our children,
Take back our Zimbabwe from these cynics,
It will be tough it won't be a picnic
It will be long, we should be strong.
Let's rewrite the books, our own testament,
Let's get ourselves out of this predicament.

The House We Sold
Troy da Costa

The inkless pages of dreamless nights we share
A poisoned history of a lost generation
One built on the broken promises of unjust gods
And watched through the mist; the beauty that could have been
How we embraced the sanctity of untruth
In hope for our handsome land
To celebrate this great house of stone built on restless sand

CHITUNGWIZA MAP (REDRAFT)
Phumulani Chipandambira

these lines are rivulets
of sewages
flowing into the Manyame river
and these are knolls
of garbages
strewn along the streets

these lines are roads
dusty and pot-holed

the big dot is a mountain
of refuse
dumped and abandoned
and these dots
denotes shacks of the illegal squatters

the red background
shows the bloodshed, the bloodshed,
the bloodshed!

Journey Home
Anesu Nyakubaya

Home is where the heart is
Mine lies down that dusty pot-hole ridden back road
In that ten hour long journey
Back to the succulence of childhood
To the carefree ways with no repercussions
Mommy always came to my rescue
She always knew how....

My heart lies by the river, where we first met
What a beauty, as natural as they come
Chocolate skinned
Perfection at its best, just the way you are
As I take this journey home
Patiently awaiting to lay my eyes on that beautiful smile of
yours....

This dead beat of a heart can't wait to reach its destination
To get away from the insanity of this concrete jungle
Away from the hustle and bustle
From this prison, this illusion of sublimity
Yet it is captivity
Bound by these unbreakable motions
In this vicious cycle...

Home is where the heart is,
Mine lies in the place I truly call home.

'Mother'

Tembi Charles

Dear 'mother'
Full of 'grace'
Your house is decked with pictures of saints,
Mother Mary and the Pope.
Rosaries in your hand,
You walk from room to room,
Murmuring the Lord's Prayer –
We hear you!

Dear 'mother'
Jesus on your tongue,
Like a Pharisee; you grace the corner of Fife Street.
And when beggars pass,
You raise your head, twisting this way and that way.
Your scraggy hand, with its pulsating veins,
Drops coins into palms.
We see you!

Dear 'mother'
Full of 'grace'
As the cock croaks,
Swish, swish, swish – goes your broom.
Below my window I hear:
'Oh the Lord my God loves me'
'With God all things are possible'
I do not stir!

Dear 'mother'
At dusk, head covered, you go into darkness.
Breaking bones, covered in soot,

You chant: 'let her die'
You scuttle back home, with a smile on your face.
Mother in law
Full of disgrace
The whole world knows!

YAHWE
Kelvin Mangwende

Rakanga ronanzva zuva makomo
Apondakaita mahwekwe nechisionekwi
Mibvunzo isinamhinduro ndakazvibvunza
Aiva munhu upi aneziso rimwechete
Chapungu chaingovaima, nekutambisa
Dundundu serechembere redafi
Kwaaienda ndakaona iri pfumvu
Ndakazvibvunzwa ndikaziva
Aiva Yahwe zvake.

The Mad Man
Interpretation by Kelvin Mangwende

The setting sapping sunshine swallowed by mountains
I met 'him' on the way to the graveyard
For the memorial service, bald headed with swollen eye
I asked myself is he a bloke?
And where was he heading? I saw him departed
In his graveyard, but his forlon shadow stood in my way.

In the Land of the Lucid
Debra Chimuka

In the land of the lucid,
Light rises in darkness.
It's not a whirlwind which took me there -
A dream could not ship me there -
There was no whirling motion
Only absence of fear.

In the land of the lucid,
Unmoved by the fear of fear
I stepped in -
It's not a whirlwind which took me there -
A dream could not ship me there -
There was no whirling motion
Only absence of fear.

In the land of the lucid,
The eye of a needle
Circles the eye,
Allowing pure observation.
It's not a whirlwind which took me there -
A dream could not ship me there -
There was no whirling motion
Only absence of fear.

In the land of the lucid,
There is lucid awareness;
That carried me from one level of awareness to another.
It's not a whirlwind which took me there -
A dream could not ship me there -
There was no whirling motion

Only absence of fear.

In the land of the lucid,
There is a rainbow of pure insight.
Rapt by visions of understanding
Limited insights tumbled down.
It's not a whirlwind which took me there -
A dream could not ship me there -
There was no whirling motion
Only absence of fear.

In the land of the lucid,
My heart became lucid.
My eyes snow-white with insight,
Limited opinions crumbled into pure insight.
It's not a whirlwind which took me there -
A dream could not ship me there -
There was no whirling motion
Only absence of fear.

In the land of the lucid,
I was transformed beyond traditional stories
The light of compassion transfigured my heart.
It's not a whirlwind which took me there -
A dream could not ship me there -
There was no whirling motion
Only absence of fear.

In the land of the lucid,
Seeing is lucid
Everything plain and beautiful.
Pure insight reigns over traditionalized insights.
It's not a whirlwind which took me there -

107

A dream could not ship me there -
There was no whirling motion
Only absence of fear.

In the land of the lucid,
There is heightened awareness
The bliss of understanding.
It's not a whirlwind which took me there -
A dream could not ship me there -
There was no whirling motion
Only absence of fear.

O come with me
To the land of the lucid...
Where pure insight exalts wisdom
Upgrading limited perceptions and self-seeking human rights
laws.
It's not a whirlwind which took me there -
A dream could not ship me there -
There was no whirling motion
Only absence of fear.

KARARA
Kelvin Mangwende

Kaipeperetswa nemhepo karara
Kainekairawo kwaienda dutu remhepo
Mhepo yakakatora nekuti kakanga
Kangova karara
Karara kakanga kakarara mumhepo
Kaimhepoirane mhepo isina mutsindo
Kari togo muchadenga ndikovate pachamweya.
Kaiva kava nemaburi kuenda kumarara kunoraswa marara

Fallen Leaf
Translation by Kelvin Mangwende

The whirlwind blew up the wilted
tattered leaves into a blazing horizon
unplugged from the shriveled stem,
the leaves melted into the raging horizon
gulped by its womb.

CANCEL
CHENJERAI MHONDERA

Cancel my name from those registered to go;
I can't go now!
For if I go now I will be in a hurry;
Let me hurray, merry and cherry;
I can't go now!
I have a task to be a sinner free before I die!
It is hell that speaks like God without mercy;
But from the list of hypocrites cancel me,
For if I go now I will be in a hurry.
I can't go now!

NDAISAZIVA KUTI NDIWO HUPENYU
Kelvin Mangwende

Dhongi rakatya chaiva chibharo
Jeri reuranda marwadzo rwaiva rwakapombwa
Nemakavi shwishwishwi mbiradzakondo
Dzikirira rakazodzikinura wani baravara kubva hope
Chekugutsa ura chaitora chitosva mwoyo wonderiri pamawere
Kukumumisodzi dikita nyakata ubvunde
Kune kaira kwaingova wokune kairamurima
Hwaiva hupenyu here kutimagadziko mhezi,
Ndaisaziva kuti ndiwo hupenyu

Not Knowing This Is Life
Translation by Kelvin Mangwende

The chain of bondage dangling in my mind
incarcerated my soulless soul to the gallows
the echoing sounds in my empty belly
Yawns of hunger, the sweat, blood and tears
Soaked my ragged garb,
exposing the nakedness of my buttocks with
the scars of war

111

On Spring Night
Learnmore Edwin Zvada

A lone Citrus lemon grew close to my grave
And it never brought me cold fruit to rot atop my headrest
But on spring night it shooed away my solitude
On whose eve I dallied with the stars and the moon
I remember ghostly effigies that ran about the edge of my grave
'Be merry within this unfit distance'
Their undulating posturing seemed to be sounding out such
tidings

In all treedom, a thorny tree called me up in carefree pomp
Tiny spring leaves carpeted the orbit around my headstone
Prickling spikelets tingled my bony frame
Coercing my extremities to scratch a fundament of knife-edge
rise
A salutation against a sullen heath ensured
As bones monkeyed about in a bath of unrestrained alacrity
And cheery again we were, my bones and I
Merrily floating in leafy cadence
Enwrapped around the notion that perhaps we weren't dead after
all

This is my Home: Sands of Time

Tendai Rinos Mwanaka

Think, think of massive, vast deep sands, those in North Africa,
and I am finding my way in these sands. Somewhere in Morocco,
not in Casablanca, not...   even in the movie. Think of the
ocean of sands, the heat, the hotness, inhospitable, as I travel
to the sea, to the rock Atlantic stuns, to get cooled in Moroccan
currents in   the
Atlantic. I see a bird, maybe a desert crow. I eye the
crow for potential, and it eyes me back. A crow
caught in the act of flying off the
desert's smiles, the desert
lends its voice to the
dead; Inhalations'
monophony and echo, blade.
I have been to a beach before, some-
where, where the warm water (the soul
is lukewarm like the heart of someone fleshly dead)
of the Indian Ocean, and the cold water of the Atlantic meets,
somewhere on the Cape coast. I am now made to think how that
doesn't compare with the sands of this desert. The calm in this
desert   is such that the sands can
be heard groaning beneath its own weight. Hot, I am-
I am chopping into the sands with my blistered feet. I think of
the sand fields, the sand   roads, the river's beaches,
sand and sand I have travelled to wherever whilst the child in me
watches, wonders in memory's house. But this sand I am seeing is
enormous amount of sand; it's sun soaked,   smug
and expanse, as I reach the beach. The beach finds me pixilated
and wanting.   But I know the beach's
weight will dissolve these clenched thoughts. Looking
back at the desert, there is sand and sand, and as my sight

grows distant to the point where the sky fingers the
land, it is revealed, reveling, no doubt,
the human…a tiny human out
there. The human; in the
arcade of bones
and joints,
going
outside, away
from the beach,
renouncing mathematics,
single mindedly developing his own
meaning. The result is more like an eye socket
laughing meaninglessly above a set of kneecaps, or nerves
forming up in order to dream. The set of kneecaps speaking to
each other eloquently of a need to collect, to fill time's spaces
with a file of memories,   each one a marker
signaling across loneliness. The flesh is sand; the flesh is dry as
you go far away from the water. The soul is water. The beach is
when the flesh and spirit just makes it. Like   when nature
is clothed in thought! But, the two are at cross purpose most of
the time,   each fighting the other by
walking off its own existence. The soul into
a region immersed in water, and the flesh in a region
inundated by sand. The sand only feels good where
it meets the water, it is at that ever shifting
thin line of the beach, and the
two are at ease with the other.
This line shifts as the flesh
and soul fights
everyday. The
soul needs
a house; it needs
the sands, just like the ocean needs

the sands (the land) for it to be an ocean, without
which it would flood everything in too much soul, like
there is such a thing as too much goodness. The beach is the line
of control, and at that point of control, the sand gives off scent in
confusion.   Like all things human,
animal, I was hungrily made- a blank hole of a thing, gaping,
arching,   which grows, me growing, wide and then
wider like a south that never fails to be struck opus of   being.
Separately the soul and flesh views a demonstration of itself to
uphold a complex melody, the more one moves away from the
beach, and thus, abruptly, it is no longer a soul or flesh. It is the
world   itself, so various, so as not to be spared as it is, as it
were, the impetus never to leave it.

Mmap New African Poets Series

If you have enjoyed *Zimbolicious Poetry Anthology Volume 2* consider these other fine books in **New African Poets Series** from *Mwanaka Media and Publishing:*

I Threw a Star in a Wine Glass by Fethi Sassi
Best New African Poets 2017 Anthology by Tendai R Mwanaka and Daniel Da Purificacao
Logbook Written by a Drifter by Tendai Rinos Mwanaka
Mad Bob Republic: Bloodlines, Bile and a Crying Child by Tendai Rinos Mwanaka
Zimbolicious Poetry Vol 1 by Tendai R Mwanaka and Edward Dzonze
Zimbolicious: An Anthology of Zimbabwean Literature and Arts, Vol 3 by Tendai Mwanaka
Under The Steel Yoke by Jabulani Mzinyathi
Fly in a Beehive by Thato Tshukudu
Bounding for Light by Richard Mbuthia
Sentiments by Jackson Matimba
Best New African Poets 2018 Anthology by Tendai R Mwanaka and Nsah Mala
Words That Matter by Gerry Sikazwe
The Ungendered by Delia Watterson
Ghetto Symphony by Mandla Mavolwane
Sky for a Foreign Bird by Fethi Sassi
A Portrait of Defiance by Tendai Rinos Mwanaka
When Escape Becomes the only Lover by Tendai R Mwanaka
ويَسهَرُ اللَّيلُ عَلى شَفَتي...وَالغَمَام by Fethi Sassi
A Letter to the President by Mbizo Chirasha

116

This is not a poem by Richard Inya
Pressed flowers by John Eppel
Righteous Indignation by Jabulani Mzinyathi:
Blooming Cactus By Mikateko Mbambo
Rhythm of Life by Olivia Ngozi Osouha
Travellers Gather Dust and Lust by Gabriel Awuah Mainoo
Chitungwiza Mushamukuru: An Anthology from Zimbabwe's Biggest Ghetto Town by Tendai Rinos Mwanaka
Because Sadness is Beautiful? by Tanaka Chidora
Of Fresh Bloom and Smoke by Abigail George
Shades of Black by Edward Dzonze

Soon to be released

Denga reshiri yokunze kwenyika by Fethi Sassi
This Body is an Empty Vessel by Beaton Galafa

https://facebook.com/MwanakaMediaAndPublishing/

Printed in the United States
by Baker & Taylor Publisher Services